50 Mexican Pizza Recipes for Home

By: Kelly Johnson

Table of Contents

Traditional Flavors:

- Classic Margherita Taco Pizza
- Salsa Verde Chicken Pizza
- Guacamole Veggie Pizza
- Chorizo and Potato Mexican Pizza
- Chorizo and Potato Mexican Pizza
- Mexican Street Corn Pizza
- Tinga de Pollo Pizza
- Pico de Gallo Shrimp Pizza
- Mole Mushroom Pizza
- Carnitas and Pineapple Pizza
- Chipotle BBQ Beef Pizza

Creative Twists:

- Mexican Breakfast Pizza
- Taco Salad Pizza
- Enchilada Pizza Rolls
- Chile Relleno Pizza
- Margarita Quesadilla Pizza
- Sopes Pizza
- Tamale Pizza
- Tostada Pizza
- Mango Habanero Chicken Pizza
- Tequila Lime Shrimp Pizza

Vegetarian and Vegan Options:

- Vegan Mexican Street Corn Pizza
- Vegetarian Fajita Pizza
- Vegan Chorizo and Potato Pizza
- Veggie Guacamole Flatbread
- Vegan Tofu Ranchero Pizza
- Cauliflower Al Pastor Pizza

- Vegan Taco Pizza
- Jackfruit Carnitas Pizza
- Vegan Chipotle BBQ Chick'n Pizza
- Mushroom and Spinach Mexican Pizza

Seafood Sensations:

- Ceviche Pizza
- Spicy Tuna Tostada Pizza
- Seafood Enchilada Pizza
- Grilled Fish Taco Pizza
- Shrimp Diablo Pizza
- Crab and Avocado Pizza
- Lobster and Mango Salsa Pizza
- Chipotle Lime Salmon Pizza
- Tuna Melt Quesadilla Pizza
- Squid Ink Seafood Pizza

Sweet Dessert Pizzas:

- Churro Dessert Pizza
- Mexican Chocolate Dessert Pizza
- Dulce de Leche Banana Pizza
- Tres Leches Fruit Pizza
- Mango Coconut Dessert Pizza
- Pineapple and Rum Raisin Dessert Pizza
- Avocado Lime Dessert Pizza
- Cajeta Apple Dessert Pizza
- Mexican Wedding Cookie Pizza
- Horchata Dessert Pizza

Traditional Flavors:

Classic Margherita Taco Pizza

Ingredients:

For the Pizza Dough:

- 1 pizza dough (store-bought or homemade)

For the Margherita Sauce:

- 1 cup tomato sauce
- 1 clove garlic, minced
- 1 teaspoon dried oregano
- Salt and pepper to taste

For the Toppings:

- 1 1/2 cups mozzarella cheese, shredded
- 2 ripe tomatoes, thinly sliced
- Fresh basil leaves
- Olive oil for drizzling

For the Taco Shell Crust:

- 6 small flour or corn tortillas
- Olive oil for brushing

Instructions:

Preparing the Taco Shell Crust:

Preheat Oven:
- Preheat your oven to 375°F (190°C).

Shape the Taco Shells:
- Lightly brush each tortilla with olive oil.
- Carefully drape each tortilla over the oven rack bars, creating a taco shell shape.
- Bake for 8-10 minutes or until the shells are crispy and golden.

Remove from Oven:
- Carefully remove the taco shells from the oven and let them cool while you prepare the other ingredients.

Preparing the Margherita Sauce:

- Make Margherita Sauce:
  - In a small bowl, mix together the tomato sauce, minced garlic, dried oregano, salt, and pepper.

Assembling the Pizza:

- Preheat Oven:
  - Adjust the oven temperature to 425°F (220°C).
- Prepare Pizza Dough:
  - Roll out the pizza dough on a floured surface to your desired thickness.
- Spread Margherita Sauce:
  - Spread the margherita sauce evenly over the pizza dough.
- Add Cheese and Tomatoes:
  - Sprinkle shredded mozzarella evenly over the sauce.
  - Arrange the sliced tomatoes on top of the cheese.
- Bake:
  - Place the pizza in the preheated oven and bake for 12-15 minutes or until the crust is golden and the cheese is melted and bubbly.
- Add Taco Shells:
  - Once the pizza is out of the oven, carefully place the pre-baked taco shells around the edge of the pizza, pressing them slightly into the crust.
- Garnish with Basil:
  - Tear fresh basil leaves and scatter them over the pizza.
- Drizzle with Olive Oil:
  - Drizzle a bit of olive oil over the entire pizza for added flavor.
- Slice and Serve:
  - Allow the pizza to cool for a few minutes, then slice and serve.

Enjoy your Classic Margherita Taco Pizza, combining the flavors of a traditional Margherita pizza with the fun and crunch of taco shells! Adjust the toppings according to your taste preferences.

Salsa Verde Chicken Pizza

Ingredients:

For the Pizza Dough:

- 1 pizza dough (store-bought or homemade)

For the Salsa Verde:

- 1 cup tomatillos, husked and chopped
- 1/2 cup white onion, chopped
- 1 jalapeño, chopped (adjust to taste)
- 2 cloves garlic, minced
- 1/4 cup fresh cilantro, chopped
- Salt and pepper to taste

For the Toppings:

- 1 1/2 cups cooked chicken, shredded
- 1 cup mozzarella cheese, shredded
- 1/2 cup red onion, thinly sliced
- 1/2 cup bell peppers (red or green), thinly sliced
- 1/4 cup black olives, sliced (optional)
- 1/4 cup fresh cilantro, chopped

Additional Garnish:

- Lime wedges for serving
- Avocado slices

Instructions:

Preparing the Salsa Verde:

Make Salsa Verde:
- In a blender or food processor, combine tomatillos, white onion, jalapeño, garlic, cilantro, salt, and pepper.
- Blend until smooth. Adjust salt and pepper to taste.

Cook Salsa Verde:
- Transfer the salsa verde to a saucepan and cook over medium heat for 8-10 minutes, stirring occasionally, until it thickens slightly. Set aside.

Assembling the Pizza:

- Preheat Oven:
  - Preheat your oven according to the pizza dough package instructions or to 425°F (220°C).
- Prepare Pizza Dough:
  - Roll out the pizza dough on a floured surface to your desired thickness.
- Spread Salsa Verde:
  - Spread a generous layer of the prepared salsa verde over the pizza dough, leaving a small border around the edges.
- Add Chicken and Toppings:
  - Distribute the shredded chicken evenly over the salsa verde.
  - Sprinkle mozzarella cheese, sliced red onion, bell peppers, and black olives (if using) over the pizza.
- Bake:
  - Place the pizza in the preheated oven and bake for 12-15 minutes or until the crust is golden and the cheese is melted and bubbly.
- Garnish:
  - Once out of the oven, sprinkle fresh cilantro over the hot pizza.
- Serve:
  - Slice the Salsa Verde Chicken Pizza into portions and serve with lime wedges and avocado slices on the side.

Enjoy the vibrant flavors of Salsa Verde combined with tender chicken on a delicious pizza crust! Adjust the spice level by controlling the amount of jalapeño in the salsa verde.

Guacamole Veggie Pizza

Ingredients:

For the Pizza Dough:

- 1 pizza dough (store-bought or homemade)

For the Guacamole:

- 3 ripe avocados
- 1 small red onion, finely diced
- 1 tomato, diced
- 1/4 cup fresh cilantro, chopped
- 1 jalapeño, finely minced (optional for heat)
- 2 cloves garlic, minced
- Juice of 1 lime
- Salt and pepper to taste

For the Toppings:

- 1 cup cherry tomatoes, halved
- 1/2 cup red bell pepper, thinly sliced
- 1/2 cup yellow bell pepper, thinly sliced
- 1/2 cup black olives, sliced
- 1/4 cup red onion, thinly sliced
- 1 cup shredded lettuce

For the Cheese:

- 1 1/2 cups shredded cheddar or Mexican blend cheese

Additional Garnish:

- Fresh cilantro, chopped
- Lime wedges for serving

Instructions:

Preparing the Guacamole:

Make Guacamole:
- In a bowl, mash the ripe avocados with a fork.

- Add diced red onion, diced tomato, chopped cilantro, minced jalapeño (if using), minced garlic, lime juice, salt, and pepper.
- Mix everything together until well combined. Adjust salt and lime juice to taste.

Assembling the Pizza:

Preheat Oven:
- Preheat your oven according to the pizza dough package instructions or to 425°F (220°C).

Prepare Pizza Dough:
- Roll out the pizza dough on a floured surface to your desired thickness.

Spread Guacamole:
- Spread a generous layer of the prepared guacamole evenly over the pizza dough, leaving a small border around the edges.

Add Toppings:
- Sprinkle shredded cheddar or Mexican blend cheese over the guacamole.
- Distribute halved cherry tomatoes, sliced red and yellow bell peppers, black olives, and sliced red onion over the pizza.

Bake:
- Place the pizza in the preheated oven and bake for 12-15 minutes or until the crust is golden and the cheese is melted and bubbly.

Garnish:
- Once out of the oven, sprinkle shredded lettuce over the hot pizza.
- Garnish with fresh chopped cilantro.

Serve:
- Slice the Guacamole Veggie Pizza into portions and serve with lime wedges on the side.

Enjoy the refreshing flavors of guacamole combined with a variety of colorful vegetables on a tasty pizza crust! Adjust the toppings according to your preference.

Chorizo and Potato Mexican Pizza

Ingredients:

For the Pizza Dough:

- 1 pizza dough (store-bought or homemade)

For the Chorizo and Potato Topping:

- 1/2 pound (225g) chorizo sausage, casing removed
- 2 medium-sized potatoes, peeled and thinly sliced
- 1 small red onion, thinly sliced
- 1 cup shredded Monterey Jack or Mexican blend cheese
- 1 tablespoon olive oil
- 1 teaspoon smoked paprika
- Salt and pepper to taste

For the Tomato Sauce:

- 1/2 cup tomato sauce
- 1 teaspoon ground cumin
- 1 teaspoon chili powder
- 1/2 teaspoon garlic powder
- Salt and pepper to taste

Additional Toppings:

- Sliced jalapeños (optional for heat)
- Fresh cilantro, chopped
- Lime wedges for serving

Instructions:

Preparing the Chorizo and Potato Topping:

Cook Chorizo:
- In a skillet over medium heat, cook the chorizo, breaking it into crumbles with a spatula, until browned. Remove excess grease if needed.

Cook Potatoes:
- In the same skillet, add thinly sliced potatoes and red onion. Cook until the potatoes are tender and the onions are translucent.
- Season with smoked paprika, salt, and pepper. Mix well.

Preparing the Tomato Sauce:

Make Tomato Sauce:
- In a small bowl, mix together tomato sauce, ground cumin, chili powder, garlic powder, salt, and pepper.

Assembling the Pizza:

Preheat Oven:
- Preheat your oven according to the pizza dough package instructions or to 425°F (220°C).

Prepare Pizza Dough:
- Roll out the pizza dough on a floured surface to your desired thickness.

Spread Tomato Sauce:
- Spread the prepared tomato sauce evenly over the pizza dough, leaving a small border around the edges.

Add Chorizo and Potato Topping:
- Evenly distribute the cooked chorizo, potato, and red onion mixture over the tomato sauce.

Sprinkle Cheese:
- Sprinkle shredded Monterey Jack or Mexican blend cheese over the toppings.

Add Optional Toppings:
- If you like it spicy, add sliced jalapeños on top.

Bake:
- Place the pizza in the preheated oven and bake for 12-15 minutes or until the crust is golden and the cheese is melted and bubbly.

Garnish:
- Once out of the oven, sprinkle fresh chopped cilantro over the hot pizza.

Serve:
- Slice the Chorizo and Potato Mexican Pizza into portions and serve with lime wedges on the side.

Enjoy the bold and savory flavors of chorizo and potatoes on this Mexican-inspired pizza! Adjust the spice level and toppings according to your taste.

Chorizo and Potato Mexican Pizza

Ingredients:

For the Pizza Dough:

- 1 pizza dough (store-bought or homemade)

For the Chorizo and Potato Topping:

- 1/2 pound (225g) chorizo sausage, casing removed
- 2 medium-sized potatoes, peeled and thinly sliced
- 1 small red onion, thinly sliced
- 1 cup shredded Monterey Jack or Mexican blend cheese
- 1 tablespoon olive oil
- 1 teaspoon smoked paprika
- Salt and pepper to taste

For the Tomato Sauce:

- 1/2 cup tomato sauce
- 1 teaspoon ground cumin
- 1 teaspoon chili powder
- 1/2 teaspoon garlic powder
- Salt and pepper to taste

Additional Toppings:

- Sliced jalapeños (optional for heat)
- Fresh cilantro, chopped
- Lime wedges for serving

Instructions:

Preparing the Chorizo and Potato Topping:

Cook Chorizo:
- In a skillet over medium heat, cook the chorizo, breaking it into crumbles with a spatula, until browned. Remove excess grease if needed.

Cook Potatoes:
- In the same skillet, add thinly sliced potatoes and red onion. Cook until the potatoes are tender and the onions are translucent.

- Season with smoked paprika, salt, and pepper. Mix well.

Preparing the Tomato Sauce:

Make Tomato Sauce:
- In a small bowl, mix together tomato sauce, ground cumin, chili powder, garlic powder, salt, and pepper.

Assembling the Pizza:

Preheat Oven:
- Preheat your oven according to the pizza dough package instructions or to 425°F (220°C).

Prepare Pizza Dough:
- Roll out the pizza dough on a floured surface to your desired thickness.

Spread Tomato Sauce:
- Spread the prepared tomato sauce evenly over the pizza dough, leaving a small border around the edges.

Add Chorizo and Potato Topping:
- Evenly distribute the cooked chorizo, potato, and red onion mixture over the tomato sauce.

Sprinkle Cheese:
- Sprinkle shredded Monterey Jack or Mexican blend cheese over the toppings.

Add Optional Toppings:
- If you like it spicy, add sliced jalapeños on top.

Bake:
- Place the pizza in the preheated oven and bake for 12-15 minutes or until the crust is golden and the cheese is melted and bubbly.

Garnish:
- Once out of the oven, sprinkle fresh chopped cilantro over the hot pizza.

Serve:
- Slice the Chorizo and Potato Mexican Pizza into portions and serve with lime wedges on the side.

Enjoy the bold and savory flavors of chorizo and potatoes on this Mexican-inspired pizza! Adjust the spice level and toppings according to your taste.

Mexican Street Corn Pizza

Ingredients:

For the Pizza Dough:

- 1 pizza dough (store-bought or homemade)

For the Mexican Street Corn Topping:

- 4 ears of corn, husked
- 1/2 cup mayonnaise
- 1/2 cup sour cream
- 1 cup cotija cheese, crumbled (or feta cheese as a substitute)
- 1 teaspoon chili powder
- 1 teaspoon smoked paprika
- 1 clove garlic, minced
- Salt and pepper to taste
- 1 tablespoon olive oil

For the Pizza Sauce:

- 1/2 cup mayonnaise
- 1 tablespoon lime juice
- 1 teaspoon chili powder
- 1 teaspoon cayenne pepper (adjust to taste)
- Salt and pepper to taste

Additional Toppings:

- 1 cup shredded mozzarella cheese
- Fresh cilantro, chopped
- Lime wedges for serving

Instructions:

Preparing the Mexican Street Corn Topping:

Grill Corn:
- Preheat a grill or grill pan over medium-high heat. Grill the corn until it's charred on all sides. Set aside to cool.

Make Street Corn Mixture:

- In a bowl, mix together mayonnaise, sour cream, crumbled cotija cheese, chili powder, smoked paprika, minced garlic, salt, and pepper.

Cut Corn Kernels:
- Once the grilled corn is cool enough to handle, cut the kernels off the cobs.

Mix Corn into Mixture:
- Fold the grilled corn kernels into the mayonnaise mixture.

Preparing the Pizza Sauce:

Make Pizza Sauce:
- In a small bowl, mix together mayonnaise, lime juice, chili powder, cayenne pepper, salt, and pepper. Adjust seasoning to taste.

Assembling the Pizza:

Preheat Oven:
- Preheat your oven according to the pizza dough package instructions or to 425°F (220°C).

Prepare Pizza Dough:
- Roll out the pizza dough on a floured surface to your desired thickness.

Spread Pizza Sauce:
- Spread the prepared spicy mayonnaise sauce evenly over the pizza dough, leaving a small border around the edges.

Add Street Corn Topping:
- Spoon the Mexican street corn mixture evenly over the pizza.

Sprinkle Cheese:
- Sprinkle shredded mozzarella cheese over the street corn topping.

Drizzle Olive Oil:
- Drizzle olive oil over the top for a golden crust.

Bake:
- Place the pizza in the preheated oven and bake for 12-15 minutes or until the crust is golden, and the cheese is melted and bubbly.

Garnish:
- Once out of the oven, sprinkle fresh chopped cilantro over the hot pizza.

Serve:
- Slice the Mexican Street Corn Pizza into portions and serve with lime wedges on the side.

Enjoy the flavors of elote in pizza form with this Mexican Street Corn Pizza! Adjust the spice level and toppings according to your preference.

Tinga de Pollo Pizza

Ingredients:

For the Pizza Dough:

- 1 pizza dough (store-bought or homemade)

For the Tinga de Pollo (Chicken Tinga):

- 1 lb (450g) boneless, skinless chicken breasts
- 1 onion, thinly sliced
- 2 cloves garlic, minced
- 1 can (14 oz) diced tomatoes
- 2 chipotle peppers in adobo sauce, chopped
- 1 teaspoon dried oregano
- 1 teaspoon ground cumin
- Salt and pepper to taste
- 2 tablespoons vegetable oil

For the Pizza Sauce:

- 1/2 cup tomato sauce
- 1 teaspoon dried oregano
- 1 teaspoon ground cumin
- Salt and pepper to taste

Additional Toppings:

- 1 cup shredded mozzarella cheese
- 1/2 cup crumbled queso fresco
- Sliced red onion
- Fresh cilantro, chopped
- Lime wedges for serving

Instructions:

Preparing the Tinga de Pollo:

Cook Chicken:

- In a pot, poach the chicken breasts in water until fully cooked. Shred the chicken using forks.

Make Tinga Sauce:

- In a skillet, heat vegetable oil over medium heat. Add sliced onions and minced garlic, sauté until softened.
- Stir in the diced tomatoes, chopped chipotle peppers, oregano, cumin, salt, and pepper. Cook for 5-7 minutes until the mixture thickens.
- Add the shredded chicken to the tinga sauce, stirring until the chicken is well coated. Simmer for an additional 10 minutes.

Preparing the Pizza Sauce:

Make Pizza Sauce:
- In a small bowl, mix together tomato sauce, dried oregano, ground cumin, salt, and pepper.

Assembling the Pizza:

Preheat Oven:
- Preheat your oven according to the pizza dough package instructions or to 425°F (220°C).

Prepare Pizza Dough:
- Roll out the pizza dough on a floured surface to your desired thickness.

Spread Pizza Sauce:
- Spread the prepared tomato sauce evenly over the pizza dough, leaving a small border around the edges.

Add Tinga de Pollo:
- Spoon the Tinga de Pollo mixture evenly over the pizza.

Sprinkle Cheeses:
- Sprinkle shredded mozzarella cheese and crumbled queso fresco over the tinga mixture.

Add Toppings:
- Scatter sliced red onions over the pizza.

Bake:
- Place the pizza in the preheated oven and bake for 12-15 minutes or until the crust is golden and the cheese is melted and bubbly.

Garnish:
- Once out of the oven, sprinkle fresh chopped cilantro over the hot pizza.

Serve:
- Slice the Tinga de Pollo Pizza into portions and serve with lime wedges on the side.

Enjoy the bold and smoky flavors of Tinga de Pollo on this unique pizza creation! Adjust the toppings and spice level according to your liking.

Pico de Gallo Shrimp Pizza

Ingredients:

For the Pizza Dough:

- 1 pizza dough (store-bought or homemade)

For the Pico de Gallo Shrimp Topping:

- 1/2 lb (225g) large shrimp, peeled and deveined
- 1 tablespoon olive oil
- 1 teaspoon smoked paprika
- Salt and pepper to taste
- 1 cup Pico de Gallo (recipe below)

For the Pico de Gallo:

- 2 cups tomatoes, diced
- 1/2 cup red onion, finely chopped
- 1/2 cup fresh cilantro, chopped
- 1 jalapeño, seeded and finely chopped
- 2 tablespoons lime juice
- Salt and pepper to taste

For the Pizza Sauce:

- 1/2 cup tomato sauce
- 1 teaspoon cumin
- 1 teaspoon chili powder
- Salt and pepper to taste

Additional Toppings:

- 1 1/2 cups shredded Monterey Jack or Mexican blend cheese
- Sliced avocado for garnish
- Fresh cilantro, chopped, for garnish
- Lime wedges for serving

Instructions:

Preparing the Pico de Gallo:

Make Pico de Gallo:
- In a bowl, combine diced tomatoes, chopped red onion, cilantro, jalapeño, lime juice, salt, and pepper.
- Mix well and set aside.

Preparing the Pizza Sauce:

Make Pizza Sauce:
- In a small bowl, mix together tomato sauce, cumin, chili powder, salt, and pepper.

Preparing the Shrimp:

Season and Cook Shrimp:
- In a bowl, toss the shrimp with olive oil, smoked paprika, salt, and pepper.
- In a skillet over medium-high heat, cook the seasoned shrimp until they turn pink and opaque. Set aside.

Assembling the Pizza:

Preheat Oven:
- Preheat your oven according to the pizza dough package instructions or to 425°F (220°C).

Prepare Pizza Dough:
- Roll out the pizza dough on a floured surface to your desired thickness.

Spread Pizza Sauce:
- Spread the prepared tomato sauce evenly over the pizza dough, leaving a small border around the edges.

Add Shrimp and Pico de Gallo:
- Distribute the cooked shrimp over the pizza.
- Spoon Pico de Gallo evenly over the pizza.

Sprinkle Cheese:
- Sprinkle shredded Monterey Jack or Mexican blend cheese over the toppings.

Bake:
- Place the pizza in the preheated oven and bake for 12-15 minutes or until the crust is golden and the cheese is melted and bubbly.

Garnish:
- Once out of the oven, garnish with sliced avocado and chopped fresh cilantro.

Serve:

- Slice the Pico de Gallo Shrimp Pizza into portions and serve with lime wedges on the side.

Enjoy the fresh and vibrant flavors of Pico de Gallo combined with succulent shrimp on this delicious pizza! Adjust the toppings according to your taste preferences.

Mole Mushroom Pizza

Ingredients:

For the Pizza Dough:

- 1 pizza dough (store-bought or homemade)

For the Mole Sauce:

- 2 tablespoons vegetable oil
- 1/2 cup chopped onion
- 2 cloves garlic, minced
- 2 tablespoons unsweetened cocoa powder
- 1 teaspoon ground cumin
- 1 teaspoon ground cinnamon
- 1/2 teaspoon chili powder
- 1/4 teaspoon cayenne pepper (adjust to taste)
- 1 can (14 oz) diced tomatoes, undrained
- 1/4 cup smooth peanut butter
- 1/4 cup raisins
- Salt and pepper to taste

For the Mushroom Topping:

- 2 cups sliced mushrooms (button or cremini)
- 1 tablespoon olive oil
- Salt and pepper to taste

For the Pizza:

- 1 1/2 cups shredded mozzarella cheese
- 1/2 cup crumbled queso fresco or feta cheese
- Fresh cilantro, chopped, for garnish
- Toasted sesame seeds, for garnish

Instructions:

Preparing the Mole Sauce:

    Sauté Onion and Garlic:

- In a saucepan, heat vegetable oil over medium heat. Sauté chopped onion and minced garlic until softened.

Make Mole Base:
- Add cocoa powder, cumin, cinnamon, chili powder, and cayenne pepper to the saucepan. Stir well to combine.

Blend Mixture:
- Add diced tomatoes (with their juices), peanut butter, and raisins to the saucepan. Blend the mixture using an immersion blender or transfer to a regular blender. Blend until smooth.

Simmer Mole:
- Simmer the mole sauce over medium-low heat for 15-20 minutes, stirring occasionally. Season with salt and pepper to taste.

Preparing the Mushroom Topping:

Sauté Mushrooms:
- In a skillet, heat olive oil over medium heat. Add sliced mushrooms and sauté until they release their moisture and become golden brown. Season with salt and pepper.

Assembling the Pizza:

Preheat Oven:
- Preheat your oven according to the pizza dough package instructions or to 425°F (220°C).

Prepare Pizza Dough:
- Roll out the pizza dough on a floured surface to your desired thickness.

Spread Mole Sauce:
- Spread a layer of the prepared mole sauce evenly over the pizza dough, leaving a small border around the edges.

Add Mushrooms and Cheese:
- Distribute the sautéed mushrooms over the mole sauce.
- Sprinkle shredded mozzarella cheese and crumbled queso fresco (or feta) over the pizza.

Bake:
- Place the pizza in the preheated oven and bake for 12-15 minutes or until the crust is golden, and the cheese is melted and bubbly.

Garnish:
- Once out of the oven, garnish with chopped fresh cilantro and toasted sesame seeds.

Serve:
- Slice the Mole Mushroom Pizza into portions and serve.

Enjoy the rich and complex flavors of mole combined with savory mushrooms on this unique and delicious pizza! Adjust the spice level and toppings according to your liking.

Carnitas and Pineapple Pizza

Ingredients:

For the Pizza Dough:

- 1 pizza dough (store-bought or homemade)

For the Carnitas:

- 1 lb (450g) pork shoulder, cut into small chunks
- 1 tablespoon vegetable oil
- 1 teaspoon ground cumin
- 1 teaspoon smoked paprika
- 1 teaspoon garlic powder
- 1 teaspoon onion powder
- Salt and pepper to taste
- 1/2 cup chicken broth

For the Pineapple Salsa:

- 1 cup diced pineapple
- 1/2 red onion, finely chopped
- 1 jalapeño, seeded and finely chopped
- 1/4 cup fresh cilantro, chopped
- Juice of 1 lime
- Salt and pepper to taste

Additional Toppings:

- 1 1/2 cups shredded Monterey Jack or Mexican blend cheese
- 1/2 cup crumbled queso fresco or feta cheese
- Sliced jalapeños (optional for heat)
- Fresh cilantro, chopped, for garnish

Instructions:

Preparing the Carnitas:

Season Pork:
- In a bowl, season the pork chunks with ground cumin, smoked paprika, garlic powder, onion powder, salt, and pepper. Toss to coat.

Sear Pork:
- Heat vegetable oil in a skillet over medium-high heat. Sear the seasoned pork until browned on all sides.

Braise Pork:
- Pour chicken broth into the skillet and bring to a simmer. Reduce heat to low, cover, and let the pork simmer until it's tender and easily shreds, about 1.5 to 2 hours. Shred the carnitas using two forks.

Preparing the Pineapple Salsa:

Make Pineapple Salsa:
- In a bowl, combine diced pineapple, chopped red onion, chopped jalapeño, chopped cilantro, lime juice, salt, and pepper. Mix well and set aside.

Assembling the Pizza:

Preheat Oven:
- Preheat your oven according to the pizza dough package instructions or to 425°F (220°C).

Prepare Pizza Dough:
- Roll out the pizza dough on a floured surface to your desired thickness.

Spread Carnitas:
- Spread the shredded carnitas evenly over the pizza dough, leaving a small border around the edges.

Add Pineapple Salsa:
- Spoon the prepared pineapple salsa over the carnitas.

Sprinkle Cheeses:
- Sprinkle shredded Monterey Jack or Mexican blend cheese and crumbled queso fresco (or feta) over the pizza.

Add Optional Toppings:
- If you like it spicy, add sliced jalapeños on top.

Bake:
- Place the pizza in the preheated oven and bake for 12-15 minutes or until the crust is golden, and the cheese is melted and bubbly.

Garnish:
- Once out of the oven, garnish with chopped fresh cilantro.

Serve:
- Slice the Carnitas and Pineapple Pizza into portions and serve.

Enjoy the savory and sweet combination of tender carnitas and juicy pineapple on this delightful pizza! Adjust the spice level and toppings according to your taste preferences.

Chipotle BBQ Beef Pizza

Ingredients:

For the Pizza Dough:

- 1 pizza dough (store-bought or homemade)

For the Chipotle BBQ Beef:

- 1 lb (450g) lean ground beef
- 1/2 cup BBQ sauce
- 2 tablespoons chipotle peppers in adobo sauce, finely chopped
- 1 tablespoon olive oil
- 1 teaspoon ground cumin
- 1 teaspoon smoked paprika
- Salt and pepper to taste

For the Pizza Sauce:

- 1/2 cup tomato sauce
- 2 tablespoons BBQ sauce
- 1 teaspoon garlic powder
- Salt and pepper to taste

Additional Toppings:

- 1 1/2 cups shredded cheddar cheese
- 1/2 cup red onion, thinly sliced
- 1/2 cup bell peppers, thinly sliced (use a mix of colors)
- Fresh cilantro, chopped, for garnish

Instructions:

Preparing the Chipotle BBQ Beef:

Cook Ground Beef:
- In a skillet over medium heat, heat olive oil. Add ground beef and cook until browned.

Add Chipotle and BBQ Sauce:

- Add chopped chipotle peppers, BBQ sauce, ground cumin, smoked paprika, salt, and pepper to the skillet. Stir to combine and let it simmer for a few minutes until the flavors meld.

Preparing the Pizza Sauce:

Make Pizza Sauce:
- In a small bowl, mix together tomato sauce, BBQ sauce, garlic powder, salt, and pepper.

Assembling the Pizza:

Preheat Oven:
- Preheat your oven according to the pizza dough package instructions or to 425°F (220°C).

Prepare Pizza Dough:
- Roll out the pizza dough on a floured surface to your desired thickness.

Spread Pizza Sauce:
- Spread the prepared BBQ-infused tomato sauce evenly over the pizza dough, leaving a small border around the edges.

Add Chipotle BBQ Beef:
- Distribute the Chipotle BBQ beef mixture evenly over the pizza.

Sprinkle Cheese and Add Toppings:
- Sprinkle shredded cheddar cheese over the beef.
- Add thinly sliced red onions and bell peppers as desired.

Bake:
- Place the pizza in the preheated oven and bake for 12-15 minutes or until the crust is golden, and the cheese is melted and bubbly.

Garnish:
- Once out of the oven, garnish with chopped fresh cilantro.

Serve:
- Slice the Chipotle BBQ Beef Pizza into portions and serve.

Enjoy the smoky and spicy flavors of chipotle-infused BBQ beef on this delicious pizza! Customize with your favorite toppings and enjoy.

Creative Twists:

Mexican Breakfast Pizza

Ingredients:

For the Pizza Dough:

- 1 pizza dough (store-bought or homemade)

For the Breakfast Pizza Toppings:

- 1 tablespoon olive oil
- 1/2 cup refried beans
- 1 cup shredded Mexican blend cheese
- 4 large eggs
- Salt and pepper to taste

For the Pico de Gallo:

- 2 cups diced tomatoes
- 1/2 cup red onion, finely chopped
- 1 jalapeño, seeded and finely chopped
- 1/4 cup fresh cilantro, chopped
- Juice of 1 lime
- Salt and pepper to taste

For Garnish:

- Avocado slices
- Sour cream
- Fresh cilantro, chopped
- Lime wedges

Instructions:

Preparing the Pico de Gallo:

   Make Pico de Gallo:
   - In a bowl, combine diced tomatoes, chopped red onion, chopped jalapeño, chopped cilantro, lime juice, salt, and pepper. Mix well and set aside.

Assembling the Breakfast Pizza:

Preheat Oven:
- Preheat your oven according to the pizza dough package instructions or to 425°F (220°C).

Prepare Pizza Dough:
- Roll out the pizza dough on a floured surface to your desired thickness.

Spread Refried Beans:
- Brush olive oil over the pizza dough. Spread a layer of refried beans evenly over the pizza, leaving a small border around the edges.

Sprinkle Cheese:
- Sprinkle shredded Mexican blend cheese over the refried beans.

Create Wells for Eggs:
- Make four small wells in the cheese and beans for the eggs.

Crack Eggs onto Pizza:
- Carefully crack an egg into each well on the pizza.

Season with Salt and Pepper:
- Season the eggs with salt and pepper to taste.

Bake:
- Place the pizza in the preheated oven and bake for 12-15 minutes or until the crust is golden, and the eggs are cooked to your liking.

Prepare Pico de Gallo:
- While the pizza is baking, you can spoon some of the prepared Pico de Gallo onto the pizza during the last few minutes of baking.

Garnish:
- Once out of the oven, garnish the breakfast pizza with avocado slices, dollops of sour cream, fresh cilantro, and lime wedges.

Serve:
- Slice the Mexican Breakfast Pizza into portions and serve.

Enjoy the flavors of a Mexican breakfast with this delicious pizza! The combination of refried beans, melted cheese, runny eggs, and fresh Pico de Gallo makes for a delightful morning treat. Customize with additional toppings to suit your taste.

Taco Salad Pizza

Ingredients:

For the Pizza Dough:

- 1 pizza dough (store-bought or homemade)

For the Taco Meat:

- 1 lb (450g) ground beef
- 1 packet taco seasoning mix
- 1/2 cup water

For the Pizza Sauce:

- 1/2 cup refried beans

For the Pizza Toppings:

- 1 cup shredded iceberg lettuce
- 1 cup diced tomatoes
- 1/2 cup shredded cheddar cheese
- 1/2 cup sliced black olives
- 1/2 cup diced red onions
- 1/4 cup chopped fresh cilantro

For Garnish:

- Sour cream
- Salsa
- Avocado slices
- Lime wedges

Instructions:

Preparing the Taco Meat:

Cook Ground Beef:
- In a skillet over medium heat, cook the ground beef until browned.

Add Taco Seasoning:
- Drain excess fat from the skillet. Add the taco seasoning mix and water. Stir well and simmer until the mixture thickens. Set aside.

Assembling the Taco Salad Pizza:

Preheat Oven:
- Preheat your oven according to the pizza dough package instructions or to 425°F (220°C).

Prepare Pizza Dough:
- Roll out the pizza dough on a floured surface to your desired thickness.

Spread Refried Beans:
- Spread a layer of refried beans evenly over the pizza dough, leaving a small border around the edges.

Add Taco Meat:
- Spread the cooked taco meat over the refried beans.

Bake:
- Place the pizza in the preheated oven and bake for 12-15 minutes or until the crust is golden.

Add Toppings:
- Once out of the oven, sprinkle shredded iceberg lettuce, diced tomatoes, shredded cheddar cheese, sliced black olives, diced red onions, and chopped fresh cilantro over the pizza.

Garnish:
- Drizzle sour cream over the top and add dollops of salsa. Garnish with avocado slices and serve with lime wedges on the side.

Slice and Serve:
- Slice the Taco Salad Pizza into portions and serve immediately.

Enjoy the vibrant and fresh flavors of a taco salad in pizza form! The combination of the seasoned taco meat, crisp veggies, and creamy toppings creates a delicious and satisfying meal. Adjust toppings and garnishes according to your preference.

Enchilada Pizza Rolls

Ingredients:

For the Enchilada Sauce:

- 2 tablespoons vegetable oil
- 2 tablespoons all-purpose flour
- 3 tablespoons chili powder
- 1 teaspoon ground cumin
- 1/2 teaspoon garlic powder
- 1/4 teaspoon onion powder
- 1/4 teaspoon dried oregano
- 2 cups chicken or vegetable broth
- Salt and pepper to taste

For the Pizza Rolls:

- 1 package (about 12) pizza dough rolls or crescent roll dough
- 1 cup cooked and shredded chicken
- 1 cup black beans, drained and rinsed
- 1 cup corn kernels (fresh, frozen, or canned)
- 1 cup shredded Mexican blend cheese
- 1/2 cup diced green onions
- 1/4 cup chopped fresh cilantro

Instructions:

Making the Enchilada Sauce:

Prepare Roux:
- In a saucepan, heat vegetable oil over medium heat. Add flour and stir to create a roux.

Add Spices:
- Stir in chili powder, ground cumin, garlic powder, onion powder, and dried oregano. Cook for about 1-2 minutes until fragrant.

Gradually Add Broth:
- Gradually whisk in chicken or vegetable broth to the roux mixture, ensuring no lumps form.

Simmer and Season:
- Bring the sauce to a simmer, stirring constantly until it thickens. Season with salt and pepper to taste. Set aside.

Preparing the Pizza Rolls:

- Preheat Oven:
  - Preheat your oven according to the pizza dough package instructions or to 375°F (190°C).
- Roll Out Dough:
  - Roll out each pizza dough roll or crescent roll into a rectangle or square on a floured surface.
- Spread Enchilada Sauce:
  - Spread a thin layer of enchilada sauce over each rolled-out dough.
- Add Filling:
  - Evenly distribute shredded chicken, black beans, corn, shredded cheese, diced green onions, and chopped cilantro over the sauce on each piece of rolled-out dough.
- Roll and Seal:
  - Carefully roll up each piece of dough, starting from one end. Seal the edges to prevent the filling from leaking out during baking.
- Slice:
  - Using a sharp knife, slice each rolled-up dough into 1-inch pizza rolls.
- Bake:
  - Place the pizza rolls on a baking sheet and bake according to the dough package instructions or until golden brown.
- Serve:
  - Once out of the oven, let them cool slightly before serving. Optionally, serve with extra enchilada sauce for dipping.

These Enchilada Pizza Rolls are a tasty fusion of enchiladas and pizza. The flavorful filling combined with the cheesy goodness makes them a great appetizer or snack. Adjust the filling ingredients to suit your preferences. Enjoy!

Chile Relleno Pizza

Ingredients:

For the Pizza Dough:

- 1 pizza dough (store-bought or homemade)

For the Chile Rellenos:

- 4 large poblano peppers
- 1 cup shredded Monterey Jack cheese
- 1 cup shredded sharp cheddar cheese
- 1/2 cup crumbled queso fresco or feta cheese
- 1 cup corn kernels (fresh, frozen, or canned)
- 1/2 cup chopped fresh cilantro
- Salt and pepper to taste

For the Egg Batter:

- 4 large eggs
- 1/2 cup all-purpose flour
- 1/2 teaspoon baking powder
- 1/2 teaspoon salt

For the Sauce:

- 1 cup tomato sauce
- 1 teaspoon ground cumin
- 1 teaspoon smoked paprika
- 1/2 teaspoon garlic powder
- Salt and pepper to taste

Additional Toppings:

- Sliced jalapeños (optional for heat)
- Avocado slices
- Lime wedges
- Sour cream for serving

Instructions:

Preparing the Chile Rellenos:

Roast and Peel Poblanos:
- Roast the poblano peppers until the skin is charred. Place them in a plastic bag to steam for a few minutes, then peel off the skins. Cut a slit along one side of each pepper and remove the seeds.

Stuff with Cheese and Corn:
- In a bowl, mix together shredded Monterey Jack, sharp cheddar, crumbled queso fresco, corn, chopped cilantro, salt, and pepper. Stuff each poblano pepper with the cheese mixture.

Making the Egg Batter:

Prepare Egg Batter:
- In a bowl, whisk together eggs, flour, baking powder, and salt until you have a smooth batter.

Preparing the Sauce:

Make Pizza Sauce:
- In a small bowl, mix together tomato sauce, ground cumin, smoked paprika, garlic powder, salt, and pepper.

Assembling the Chile Relleno Pizza:

Preheat Oven:
- Preheat your oven according to the pizza dough package instructions or to 425°F (220°C).

Prepare Pizza Dough:
- Roll out the pizza dough on a floured surface to your desired thickness.

Spread Sauce:
- Spread a layer of the prepared pizza sauce evenly over the pizza dough, leaving a small border around the edges.

Arrange Stuffed Poblanos:
- Arrange the stuffed poblano peppers on top of the pizza sauce.

Pour Egg Batter:
- Pour the egg batter over and around the stuffed poblanos, allowing it to spread across the pizza.

Bake:
- Place the pizza in the preheated oven and bake for 15-20 minutes or until the crust is golden, and the egg batter is set.

Optional Toppings:
- Add sliced jalapeños for extra heat, if desired.

Garnish and Serve:

- Once out of the oven, garnish the Chile Relleno Pizza with avocado slices and chopped cilantro. Serve with lime wedges and sour cream on the side.

Enjoy the unique and flavorful combination of Chile Rellenos on a pizza crust! The cheesy and slightly spicy filling, along with the eggy texture, makes for a delicious and satisfying dish. Adjust the spice level and toppings according to your preference.

Margarita Quesadilla Pizza

Ingredients:

For the Quesadilla Base:

- 2 large flour tortillas
- 1 cup shredded mozzarella cheese
- 1 cup cherry tomatoes, halved
- 1/4 cup fresh basil leaves, torn
- Olive oil for brushing

For the Margarita Toppings:

- 1 cup tomato sauce
- 1 cup fresh mozzarella, sliced
- 2 tablespoons grated Parmesan cheese
- 1/4 cup fresh basil leaves, torn
- Salt and pepper to taste

Optional Garnish:

- Balsamic glaze
- Red pepper flakes

Instructions:

Preparing the Quesadilla Base:

Preheat Oven:
- Preheat your oven to 400°F (200°C).

Assemble Quesadilla:

- Place one flour tortilla on a baking sheet. Sprinkle half of the shredded mozzarella evenly over the tortilla. Arrange the halved cherry tomatoes and torn basil leaves on top. Place the second tortilla on top.

Brush with Olive Oil:
- Lightly brush the top tortilla with olive oil.

Bake:
- Bake in the preheated oven for 8-10 minutes or until the cheese is melted, and the tortillas are golden and crispy.

Remove and Set Aside:
- Remove the quesadilla base from the oven and set aside.

Assembling the Margarita Toppings:

Spread Tomato Sauce:
- Spread tomato sauce evenly over the baked quesadilla base.

Add Fresh Mozzarella:
- Arrange sliced fresh mozzarella on top of the tomato sauce.

Sprinkle Parmesan:
- Sprinkle grated Parmesan cheese over the mozzarella.

Season and Add Basil:
- Season with salt and pepper to taste. Scatter torn basil leaves over the pizza.

Bake Again:
- Return the pizza to the oven and bake for an additional 10-12 minutes or until the cheese is bubbly, and the crust is crispy.

Optional Garnish:
- Drizzle balsamic glaze over the pizza for added flavor. Sprinkle red pepper flakes if you like a bit of heat.

Slice and Serve:
- Once out of the oven, let the Margarita Quesadilla Pizza cool slightly before slicing. Serve warm.

Enjoy this fusion of quesadilla and Margarita pizza flavors! The crispy tortilla crust, gooey cheese, and fresh tomato-basil topping create a delightful combination. Customize the toppings and garnishes to suit your taste preferences.

Sopes Pizza

Ingredients:

For the Quesadilla "Crust":

- 4 large flour tortillas
- 2 cups shredded mozzarella cheese
- 1 cup cherry tomatoes, sliced
- Fresh basil leaves, torn
- Olive oil for brushing

For the Margarita Toppings:

- 1 cup tomato sauce
- 1 cup fresh mozzarella, sliced
- Fresh basil leaves, torn
- Salt and pepper to taste
- Balsamic glaze (optional for drizzling)

Instructions:

Preparing the Quesadilla "Crust":

Preheat Oven:
- Preheat your oven to 425°F (220°C).

Assemble Quesadilla Layers:
- Place one tortilla on a baking sheet. Sprinkle a layer of shredded mozzarella cheese, followed by sliced cherry tomatoes and torn basil leaves. Top with another tortilla.

Repeat for Second Quesadilla:
- Repeat the process to create a second quesadilla on the baking sheet.

Brush with Olive Oil:
- Lightly brush the top of each quesadilla with olive oil.

Bake:
- Bake in the preheated oven for about 10-12 minutes or until the cheese is melted, and the tortillas are golden and crispy.

Preparing the Margarita Toppings:

Assemble Margarita Pizza:

- Once the quesadillas are out of the oven, spread a layer of tomato sauce over each quesadilla. Add slices of fresh mozzarella and torn basil leaves on top.

Season with Salt and Pepper:
- Season with salt and pepper to taste.

Optional Balsamic Glaze:
- If desired, drizzle with balsamic glaze for an extra touch of flavor.

Broil:
- Set your oven to broil and place the margarita pizzas under the broiler for 2-3 minutes or until the cheese is bubbly and slightly browned.

Slice and Serve:
- Remove from the oven, let it cool for a minute, then slice into wedges.

Enjoy the Margarita Quesadilla Pizza with the perfect blend of Italian and Mexican flavors! The crispy quesadilla crust paired with the classic margarita pizza toppings creates a delicious fusion dish. Serve it as an appetizer or main course. Adjust the toppings and drizzles according to your preference.

Tamale Pizza

Ingredients:

For the Tamale "Crust":

- 2 cups masa harina (corn flour)
- 1 1/2 cups chicken or vegetable broth
- 1/2 cup vegetable oil or melted lard
- 1 teaspoon baking powder
- 1/2 teaspoon salt

For the Pizza Toppings:

- 1 cup red or green enchilada sauce
- 2 cups cooked and shredded chicken
- 1 cup black beans, drained and rinsed
- 1 cup corn kernels (fresh, frozen, or canned)
- 1 cup shredded Mexican blend cheese
- Sliced jalapeños (optional for heat)
- Chopped fresh cilantro for garnish

Instructions:

Making the Tamale "Crust":

Preheat Oven:
- Preheat your oven to 400°F (200°C).

Prepare Tamale Dough:
- In a large bowl, mix masa harina, chicken or vegetable broth, vegetable oil or melted lard, baking powder, and salt until a soft dough forms.

Spread Tamale Dough:
- Press the tamale dough evenly onto a pizza stone or a baking sheet, forming a thin crust.

Bake:
- Bake the tamale crust in the preheated oven for about 10-12 minutes or until it sets and edges start to lightly brown.

Assembling the Tamale Pizza:

Spread Enchilada Sauce:

- Remove the tamale crust from the oven and spread a layer of red or green enchilada sauce over the crust.

Add Chicken and Toppings:
- Evenly distribute the shredded chicken, black beans, corn kernels, and shredded Mexican blend cheese over the enchilada sauce.

Optional Jalapeños:
- If you like it spicy, add sliced jalapeños on top.

Bake Again:
- Return the tamale pizza to the oven and bake for an additional 12-15 minutes or until the cheese is melted and bubbly.

Garnish:
- Once out of the oven, garnish with chopped fresh cilantro.

Slice and Serve:
- Slice the Tamale Pizza into wedges and serve warm.

Enjoy the unique twist of tamale flavors in a pizza format! The tamale crust provides a delicious and hearty base for your favorite Mexican-inspired toppings. Customize the toppings according to your taste preferences.

Tostada Pizza

Ingredients:

For the Pizza Crust:

- 1 pizza dough (store-bought or homemade)

For the Refried Beans:

- 1 can (15 oz) black or pinto beans, drained and rinsed
- 1 tablespoon vegetable oil
- 1/2 onion, finely chopped
- 2 cloves garlic, minced
- 1 teaspoon ground cumin
- Salt and pepper to taste

For the Tostada Pizza Toppings:

- 1 cup cooked and shredded chicken or beef (seasoned with taco seasoning)
- 1 cup shredded lettuce
- 1 cup diced tomatoes
- 1 cup shredded Mexican blend cheese
- 1/2 cup sliced black olives
- 1/4 cup chopped fresh cilantro
- Sliced jalapeños (optional for heat)

For the Avocado Cream Sauce:

- 1 ripe avocado
- 1/4 cup sour cream
- 1 tablespoon lime juice
- Salt and pepper to taste

Instructions:

Preparing the Refried Beans:

    Cook Beans:
- In a pan, heat vegetable oil over medium heat. Add chopped onions and garlic, sauté until softened.

    Add Beans and Spices:

- Add the drained beans to the pan. Mash them with a fork or potato masher. Stir in ground cumin, salt, and pepper. Cook until heated through and well combined. Set aside.

Making the Avocado Cream Sauce:

Prepare Avocado Cream:
- In a blender or food processor, combine ripe avocado, sour cream, lime juice, salt, and pepper. Blend until smooth. Adjust the consistency by adding more lime juice or water if needed.

Assembling the Tostada Pizza:

Preheat Oven:
- Preheat your oven according to the pizza dough package instructions or to 425°F (220°C).

Roll Out Pizza Dough:
- Roll out the pizza dough on a floured surface to your desired thickness.

Spread Refried Beans:
- Spread a layer of the prepared refried beans over the pizza dough, leaving a small border around the edges.

Add Shredded Chicken/Beef:
- Evenly distribute the seasoned and shredded chicken or beef over the refried beans.

Sprinkle Cheese:
- Sprinkle shredded Mexican blend cheese over the pizza.

Bake:
- Place the pizza in the preheated oven and bake for 12-15 minutes or until the crust is golden, and the cheese is melted and bubbly.

Add Fresh Toppings:
- Once out of the oven, top the pizza with shredded lettuce, diced tomatoes, sliced black olives, chopped cilantro, and sliced jalapeños if desired.

Drizzle with Avocado Cream:
- Drizzle the avocado cream sauce over the pizza.

Slice and Serve:
- Slice the Tostada Pizza into portions and serve immediately.

Enjoy the combination of classic tostada toppings on a pizza crust! The refried beans, seasoned meat, fresh veggies, and creamy avocado sauce make for a flavorful and satisfying meal. Adjust the toppings and spice level according to your preference.

Mango Habanero Chicken Pizza

Ingredients:

For the Pizza:

- 1 pizza dough (store-bought or homemade)
- 1 cup cooked and shredded chicken breast
- 1 cup diced mango
- 1/2 cup sliced red onion
- 1/2 cup sliced bell peppers (any color)
- 1 cup shredded mozzarella cheese
- 1/2 cup crumbled feta cheese
- Fresh cilantro for garnish

For the Mango Habanero Sauce:

- 1 cup diced mango
- 2 habanero peppers, seeds removed (adjust to taste)
- 2 tablespoons honey
- 2 tablespoons apple cider vinegar
- 1 tablespoon olive oil
- Salt to taste

Instructions:

Making the Mango Habanero Sauce:

    Prepare Mango Habanero Sauce:
- In a blender or food processor, combine diced mango, habanero peppers, honey, apple cider vinegar, olive oil, and a pinch of salt. Blend until smooth. Adjust the sweetness and spiciness to your liking.

Assembling the Mango Habanero Chicken Pizza:

    Preheat Oven:
- Preheat your oven according to the pizza dough package instructions or to 425°F (220°C).

    Roll Out Pizza Dough:
- Roll out the pizza dough on a floured surface to your desired thickness.

    Spread Mango Habanero Sauce:

- Spread a generous layer of the prepared Mango Habanero Sauce over the pizza dough, leaving a small border around the edges.

Add Shredded Chicken and Toppings:
- Evenly distribute the shredded chicken, diced mango, sliced red onion, and sliced bell peppers over the sauce.

Sprinkle Cheeses:
- Sprinkle shredded mozzarella and crumbled feta cheese over the pizza.

Bake:
- Place the pizza in the preheated oven and bake for 12-15 minutes or until the crust is golden, and the cheese is melted and bubbly.

Garnish and Serve:
- Once out of the oven, garnish the Mango Habanero Chicken Pizza with fresh cilantro. Slice into portions and serve immediately.

Enjoy the sweet and spicy kick of Mango Habanero Chicken Pizza! The combination of juicy mango, spicy habanero, and savory chicken creates a flavor-packed pizza. Adjust the spice level by adding more or fewer habanero peppers based on your preference.

Tequila Lime Shrimp Pizza

Ingredients:

For the Pizza:

- 1 pizza dough (store-bought or homemade)
- 1 cup cooked and peeled shrimp, chopped
- 1/2 cup red bell pepper, thinly sliced
- 1/2 cup red onion, thinly sliced
- 1 cup shredded mozzarella cheese
- 1/2 cup crumbled feta cheese
- Fresh cilantro for garnish

For the Tequila Lime Marinade:

- 2 tablespoons tequila
- Zest and juice of 2 limes
- 2 tablespoons olive oil
- 2 cloves garlic, minced
- 1 teaspoon honey
- Salt and pepper to taste

For the Avocado Crema:

- 1 ripe avocado
- 1/4 cup sour cream
- 1 tablespoon lime juice
- Salt and pepper to taste

Instructions:

Making the Tequila Lime Marinade:

    Prepare Tequila Lime Marinade:
- In a bowl, whisk together tequila, lime zest, lime juice, olive oil, minced garlic, honey, salt, and pepper. Set aside.

    Marinate Shrimp:
- Place the chopped shrimp in a bowl and pour half of the tequila lime marinade over them. Toss to coat evenly and let it marinate for at least 15 minutes.

Making the Avocado Crema:

Prepare Avocado Crema:
- In a blender or food processor, blend together ripe avocado, sour cream, lime juice, salt, and pepper until smooth. Adjust the consistency with additional lime juice or water if needed.

Assembling the Tequila Lime Shrimp Pizza:

Preheat Oven:
- Preheat your oven according to the pizza dough package instructions or to 425°F (220°C).

Roll Out Pizza Dough:
- Roll out the pizza dough on a floured surface to your desired thickness.

Spread Tequila Lime Shrimp:
- Spread the marinated shrimp evenly over the pizza dough, along with sliced red bell pepper and red onion.

Sprinkle Cheeses:
- Sprinkle shredded mozzarella and crumbled feta cheese over the pizza.

Bake:
- Place the pizza in the preheated oven and bake for 12-15 minutes or until the crust is golden, and the cheese is melted and bubbly.

Garnish and Serve:
- Once out of the oven, drizzle the remaining tequila lime marinade over the pizza, garnish with fresh cilantro, and serve slices with dollops of avocado crema.

Enjoy the vibrant flavors of Tequila Lime Shrimp Pizza! The zesty marinade, succulent shrimp, and creamy avocado crema make for a refreshing and delicious pizza. Adjust the lime and tequila quantities according to your taste preferences.

Vegetarian and Vegan Options:

Vegan Mexican Street Corn Pizza

Ingredients:

For the Pizza:

- 1 pizza dough (store-bought or homemade)
- 1 cup canned corn kernels, drained
- 1/2 cup vegan mayonnaise
- 2 tablespoons nutritional yeast
- 1 tablespoon lime juice
- 1 teaspoon chili powder
- 1/2 teaspoon garlic powder
- Salt and pepper to taste
- 1 cup cherry tomatoes, halved
- 1/4 cup chopped fresh cilantro
- 1/4 cup sliced green onions

For the Cashew Cotija Cheese:

- 1 cup raw cashews, soaked in hot water for at least 2 hours
- 2 tablespoons nutritional yeast
- 1 tablespoon apple cider vinegar
- 1/2 teaspoon salt

Instructions:

Making the Cashew Cotija Cheese:

Prepare Cashew Cotija Cheese:
- In a blender or food processor, combine soaked cashews, nutritional yeast, apple cider vinegar, and salt. Blend until smooth and resembling the texture of crumbly cotija cheese. Set aside.

Making the Mexican Street Corn Sauce:

Prepare Mexican Street Corn Sauce:

- In a bowl, mix together vegan mayonnaise, nutritional yeast, lime juice, chili powder, garlic powder, salt, and pepper. This will be your Mexican street corn sauce.

Assembling the Vegan Mexican Street Corn Pizza:

Preheat Oven:
- Preheat your oven according to the pizza dough package instructions or to 425°F (220°C).

Roll Out Pizza Dough:
- Roll out the pizza dough on a floured surface to your desired thickness.

Spread Corn Sauce:
- Spread a layer of the Mexican street corn sauce over the pizza dough, leaving a small border around the edges.

Sprinkle Corn Kernels:
- Evenly distribute the canned corn kernels over the sauce.

Add Cherry Tomatoes and Cashew Cotija:
- Scatter halved cherry tomatoes over the pizza. Crumble the prepared cashew cotija cheese on top.

Bake:
- Place the pizza in the preheated oven and bake for 12-15 minutes or until the crust is golden, and the toppings are heated through.

Garnish and Serve:
- Once out of the oven, garnish the Vegan Mexican Street Corn Pizza with chopped fresh cilantro and sliced green onions. Slice into portions and serve.

Enjoy the delicious flavors of Mexican street corn in a vegan pizza format! The creamy corn sauce, tangy cashew cotija cheese, and fresh toppings create a satisfying and plant-based meal. Adjust the seasonings and toppings according to your taste preferences.

Vegetarian Fajita Pizza

Ingredients:

For the Pizza:

- 1 pizza dough (store-bought or homemade)
- 1 cup black beans, cooked and drained
- 1 bell pepper, thinly sliced (any color)
- 1 red onion, thinly sliced
- 1 cup corn kernels (fresh, frozen, or canned)
- 1 cup shredded Monterey Jack or Mexican blend cheese
- 1 tablespoon olive oil
- Salt and pepper to taste

For the Fajita Seasoning:

- 1 teaspoon chili powder
- 1/2 teaspoon cumin
- 1/2 teaspoon paprika
- 1/4 teaspoon garlic powder
- 1/4 teaspoon onion powder
- Salt and pepper to taste

For the Toppings:

- Fresh cilantro, chopped
- Avocado slices
- Lime wedges
- Salsa or hot sauce (optional)

Instructions:

Preparing the Fajita Vegetables:

Preheat Oven:
- Preheat your oven according to the pizza dough package instructions or to 425°F (220°C).

Slice Vegetables:
- In a bowl, toss the bell pepper and red onion slices with olive oil, salt, and pepper.

Fajita Seasoning:
- Sprinkle the fajita seasoning over the vegetables and toss until well coated.

Roast Vegetables:
- Spread the seasoned vegetables on a baking sheet and roast in the preheated oven for about 15-20 minutes or until they are tender and slightly charred.

Assembling the Vegetarian Fajita Pizza:

Roll Out Pizza Dough:
- Roll out the pizza dough on a floured surface to your desired thickness.

Prebake Dough (Optional):
- If desired, you can prebake the pizza dough for 5-7 minutes to ensure a crisp crust.

Spread Black Beans:
- Spread the cooked black beans over the pizza dough.

Arrange Fajita Vegetables:
- Arrange the roasted fajita vegetables evenly over the black beans.

Sprinkle Cheese:
- Sprinkle shredded Monterey Jack or Mexican blend cheese over the vegetables.

Bake:
- Place the pizza in the preheated oven and bake for 12-15 minutes or until the crust is golden, and the cheese is melted and bubbly.

Garnish and Serve:
- Once out of the oven, garnish the Vegetarian Fajita Pizza with fresh cilantro. Serve slices with avocado slices, lime wedges, and salsa or hot sauce if desired.

Enjoy the flavors of fajitas on a delicious pizza crust! This Vegetarian Fajita Pizza is loaded with roasted vegetables, black beans, and gooey cheese. Customize the toppings and seasonings to suit your taste preferences.

Vegan Chorizo and Potato Pizza

Ingredients:

For the Pizza Dough:

- 1 pizza dough (store-bought or homemade)

For the Vegan Chorizo:

- 1 cup textured vegetable protein (TVP)
- 1 cup hot water
- 2 tablespoons tomato paste
- 1 tablespoon soy sauce
- 1 teaspoon smoked paprika
- 1 teaspoon ground cumin
- 1/2 teaspoon chili powder
- 1/2 teaspoon garlic powder
- 1/2 teaspoon onion powder
- 1/4 teaspoon cayenne pepper (optional, for heat)
- Salt and pepper to taste
- 2 tablespoons vegetable oil, for cooking

For the Potato Topping:

- 1 large potato, peeled and thinly sliced
- 1 tablespoon olive oil
- Salt and pepper to taste

For the Pizza Sauce:

- 1/2 cup tomato sauce
- 1 teaspoon dried oregano
- 1/2 teaspoon garlic powder
- Salt and pepper to taste

For the Vegan Cheese (Optional):

- Vegan mozzarella or any plant-based cheese of your choice

Additional Toppings:

- Sliced red onions

- Fresh cilantro, chopped
- Avocado slices

Instructions:

Making the Vegan Chorizo:

Rehydrate TVP:
- In a bowl, combine the textured vegetable protein (TVP) with hot water. Let it sit for 5-10 minutes until fully rehydrated.

Prepare Chorizo Mixture:
- In a separate bowl, mix together the rehydrated TVP, tomato paste, soy sauce, smoked paprika, ground cumin, chili powder, garlic powder, onion powder, cayenne pepper (if using), salt, and pepper.

Cook Chorizo:
- Heat vegetable oil in a skillet over medium heat. Add the chorizo mixture and cook for 8-10 minutes, stirring occasionally, until it's browned and flavorful. Set aside.

Preparing the Potato Topping:

Preheat Oven:
- Preheat your oven according to the pizza dough package instructions or to 425°F (220°C).

Coat Potatoes:
- In a bowl, toss the thinly sliced potatoes with olive oil, salt, and pepper.

Bake Potatoes:
- Spread the seasoned potato slices on a baking sheet and bake in the preheated oven for about 15-20 minutes or until they are tender and slightly crispy.

Making the Pizza Sauce:

Prepare Pizza Sauce:
- In a bowl, mix together tomato sauce, dried oregano, garlic powder, salt, and pepper.

Assembling the Vegan Chorizo and Potato Pizza:

Roll Out Pizza Dough:
- Roll out the pizza dough on a floured surface to your desired thickness.

Spread Pizza Sauce:
- Spread a layer of the prepared pizza sauce over the pizza dough.

Add Vegan Chorizo and Potatoes:
- Evenly distribute the cooked vegan chorizo and baked potato slices over the pizza.

Optional Vegan Cheese:
- If using vegan cheese, sprinkle it over the toppings.

Bake:
- Place the pizza in the preheated oven and bake for 12-15 minutes or until the crust is golden, and the toppings are heated through.

Garnish and Serve:
- Once out of the oven, garnish the Vegan Chorizo and Potato Pizza with sliced red onions, chopped fresh cilantro, and avocado slices. Slice and serve.

Enjoy the delicious and flavorful Vegan Chorizo and Potato Pizza! This plant-based pizza is loaded with savory vegan chorizo, crispy potatoes, and a variety of tasty toppings. Adjust the spice level and toppings according to your preference.

Veggie Guacamole Flatbread

Ingredients:

For the Flatbread:

- 2 whole wheat flatbreads or naan bread
- 2 tablespoons olive oil
- 1 teaspoon garlic powder
- Salt and pepper to taste

For the Veggie Guacamole:

- 2 ripe avocados, mashed
- 1 medium tomato, diced
- 1/2 red onion, finely chopped
- 1/4 cup fresh cilantro, chopped
- 1 jalapeño, seeded and finely chopped (optional for heat)
- 1 clove garlic, minced
- Juice of 1 lime
- Salt and pepper to taste

Additional Toppings:

- 1 cup mixed greens (e.g., arugula, spinach)
- 1/2 cup cherry tomatoes, halved
- 1/4 cup sliced radishes
- 1/4 cup crumbled feta cheese (optional)

Instructions:

Preparing the Flatbread:

Preheat Oven:
- Preheat your oven according to the flatbread or naan package instructions or to 400°F (200°C).

Brush with Olive Oil:
- Brush each flatbread with olive oil on both sides. Sprinkle with garlic powder, salt, and pepper.

Bake Flatbreads:
- Place the flatbreads directly on the oven rack or a baking sheet and bake for 5-7 minutes or until they are golden and crispy.

Making the Veggie Guacamole:

Prepare Guacamole:
- In a bowl, combine the mashed avocados, diced tomatoes, chopped red onion, cilantro, jalapeño (if using), minced garlic, lime juice, salt, and pepper. Mix until well combined.

Assembling the Veggie Guacamole Flatbread:

Spread Guacamole:
- Spread a generous layer of the veggie guacamole over each baked flatbread.

Add Greens and Toppings:
- Top the guacamole with mixed greens, halved cherry tomatoes, sliced radishes, and crumbled feta cheese (if using).

Slice and Serve:
- Slice the Veggie Guacamole Flatbread into portions and serve immediately.

Enjoy the freshness and vibrant flavors of this Veggie Guacamole Flatbread! It's a perfect combination of creamy guacamole, crisp flatbread, and a variety of colorful toppings. Customize the toppings based on your preferences, and feel free to add a drizzle of hot sauce or additional lime juice for extra zing.

Vegan Tofu Ranchero Pizza

Ingredients:

For the Pizza Dough:

- 1 pizza dough (store-bought or homemade)

For the Tofu Ranchero:

- 1 block extra-firm tofu, pressed and crumbled
- 1 tablespoon olive oil
- 1 medium onion, finely chopped
- 2 cloves garlic, minced
- 1 bell pepper, diced
- 1 teaspoon ground cumin
- 1 teaspoon chili powder
- 1/2 teaspoon smoked paprika
- Salt and pepper to taste
- 1 cup tomato sauce or pizza sauce

Additional Toppings:

- 1 cup corn kernels (fresh, frozen, or canned)
- 1/2 cup black beans, cooked and drained
- 1 cup vegan cheese (cheddar or Mexican blend)
- Sliced jalapeños (optional for heat)
- Fresh cilantro, chopped

For Serving:

- Avocado slices
- Lime wedges

Instructions:

Preparing the Tofu Ranchero:

Press Tofu:
- Press the extra-firm tofu to remove excess water, then crumble it into small pieces.

Cook Tofu Mixture:

- In a skillet, heat olive oil over medium heat. Add chopped onions, minced garlic, and diced bell pepper. Sauté until the vegetables are softened.

Add Tofu and Spices:
- Add the crumbled tofu to the skillet. Season with ground cumin, chili powder, smoked paprika, salt, and pepper. Cook for 5-7 minutes, stirring occasionally, until the tofu is well-cooked and has absorbed the flavors.

Add Tomato Sauce:
- Pour in the tomato sauce or pizza sauce, and mix well. Allow the mixture to simmer for an additional 5 minutes. Adjust seasoning if necessary.

Assembling the Vegan Tofu Ranchero Pizza:

Preheat Oven:
- Preheat your oven according to the pizza dough package instructions or to 425°F (220°C).

Roll Out Pizza Dough:
- Roll out the pizza dough on a floured surface to your desired thickness.

Spread Tofu Ranchero Mixture:
- Spread the prepared Tofu Ranchero mixture evenly over the pizza dough.

Add Corn, Black Beans, and Vegan Cheese:
- Sprinkle corn kernels and black beans over the tofu mixture. Top with vegan cheese.

Optional Jalapeños:
- If you like it spicy, add sliced jalapeños on top.

Bake:
- Place the pizza in the preheated oven and bake for 12-15 minutes or until the crust is golden, and the cheese is melted and bubbly.

Garnish and Serve:
- Once out of the oven, garnish the Vegan Tofu Ranchero Pizza with fresh cilantro. Serve slices with avocado slices and lime wedges.

Enjoy the savory and spicy flavors of this Vegan Tofu Ranchero Pizza! The crumbled tofu provides a satisfying texture, and the combination of spices and toppings makes for a delicious and hearty vegan pizza. Adjust the spice level and toppings according to your taste preference.

Cauliflower Al Pastor Pizza

Ingredients:

For the Pizza Dough:

- 1 pizza dough (store-bought or homemade)

For the Cauliflower Al Pastor:

- 1 small cauliflower, cut into small florets
- 1/2 cup diced pineapple
- 1/2 red onion, thinly sliced
- 2 tablespoons achiote paste
- 2 tablespoons pineapple juice
- 1 tablespoon apple cider vinegar
- 1 tablespoon olive oil
- 1 teaspoon ground cumin
- 1 teaspoon dried oregano
- 1/2 teaspoon smoked paprika
- Salt and pepper to taste
- 1 tablespoon chopped fresh cilantro (for garnish)

Additional Toppings:

- 1 cup vegan mozzarella or any plant-based cheese of your choice
- Sliced jalapeños (optional for heat)
- Lime wedges (for serving)

For the Cilantro-Lime Crema:

- 1/2 cup vegan sour cream
- 2 tablespoons chopped fresh cilantro
- 1 tablespoon lime juice
- Salt and pepper to taste

Instructions:

Preparing the Cauliflower Al Pastor:

    Marinate Cauliflower:

- In a bowl, combine achiote paste, pineapple juice, apple cider vinegar, olive oil, ground cumin, dried oregano, smoked paprika, salt, and pepper. Mix well to create the marinade.

Coat Cauliflower:
- Toss the cauliflower florets in the marinade until evenly coated. Allow the cauliflower to marinate for at least 30 minutes.

Roast Cauliflower:
- Preheat your oven to 425°F (220°C). Spread the marinated cauliflower on a baking sheet and roast for 20-25 minutes or until the edges are golden and crispy.

Making the Cilantro-Lime Crema:

Prepare Cilantro-Lime Crema:
- In a small bowl, mix together vegan sour cream, chopped cilantro, lime juice, salt, and pepper. Adjust the flavors according to your taste.

Assembling the Cauliflower Al Pastor Pizza:

Preheat Oven:
- Preheat your oven according to the pizza dough package instructions or to 425°F (220°C).

Roll Out Pizza Dough:
- Roll out the pizza dough on a floured surface to your desired thickness.

Spread Vegan Cheese:
- Spread a layer of vegan mozzarella or your chosen plant-based cheese over the pizza dough.

Add Cauliflower Al Pastor:
- Distribute the roasted cauliflower al pastor evenly over the cheese. Add diced pineapple and thinly sliced red onion.

Optional Jalapeños:
- If you like it spicy, add sliced jalapeños on top.

Bake:
- Place the pizza in the preheated oven and bake for 12-15 minutes or until the crust is golden, and the cheese is melted and bubbly.

Drizzle with Cilantro-Lime Crema:
- Once out of the oven, drizzle the pizza with the prepared cilantro-lime crema. Sprinkle chopped fresh cilantro on top.

Serve:

- Slice the Cauliflower Al Pastor Pizza and serve with lime wedges on the side.

Enjoy the unique and flavorful combination of Cauliflower Al Pastor Pizza! The roasted cauliflower, pineapple, and aromatic spices create a delicious plant-based twist on the classic al pastor flavor. Customize the toppings and adjust the spice level to suit your taste.

Vegan Taco Pizza

Ingredients:

For the Pizza Dough:

- 1 pizza dough (store-bought or homemade)

For the Vegan Taco "Meat":

- 1 cup cooked and crumbled textured vegetable protein (TVP) or cooked lentils
- 1 tablespoon olive oil
- 1 small onion, finely chopped
- 2 cloves garlic, minced
- 1 packet taco seasoning (or homemade blend)
- 1/4 cup tomato sauce
- Salt and pepper to taste

For the Pizza Sauce:

- 1/2 cup tomato sauce
- 1 teaspoon dried oregano
- 1/2 teaspoon garlic powder
- Salt and pepper to taste

Additional Toppings:

- 1 cup shredded lettuce
- 1 cup diced tomatoes
- 1 cup diced bell peppers (any color)
- 1 cup corn kernels (fresh, frozen, or canned)
- 1 cup shredded vegan cheese (cheddar or Mexican blend)

For Garnish:

- Sliced jalapeños (optional for heat)
- Fresh cilantro, chopped
- Avocado slices
- Vegan sour cream or salsa (optional)

Instructions:

Preparing the Vegan Taco "Meat":

Cook Taco "Meat":
- In a skillet, heat olive oil over medium heat. Add chopped onions and minced garlic. Sauté until softened.

Add Textured Vegetable Protein (TVP) or Lentils:
- Add the cooked and crumbled TVP or cooked lentils to the skillet. Stir in taco seasoning, tomato sauce, salt, and pepper. Cook for an additional 5-7 minutes until well combined and heated through.

Making the Pizza Sauce:

Prepare Pizza Sauce:
- In a bowl, mix together tomato sauce, dried oregano, garlic powder, salt, and pepper.

Assembling the Vegan Taco Pizza:

Preheat Oven:
- Preheat your oven according to the pizza dough package instructions or to 425°F (220°C).

Roll Out Pizza Dough:
- Roll out the pizza dough on a floured surface to your desired thickness.

Spread Pizza Sauce:
- Spread a layer of the prepared pizza sauce over the pizza dough.

Add Vegan Taco "Meat" and Toppings:
- Evenly distribute the vegan taco "meat" over the pizza sauce. Top with shredded lettuce, diced tomatoes, diced bell peppers, corn, and shredded vegan cheese.

Optional Jalapeños:
- If you like it spicy, add sliced jalapeños on top.

Bake:
- Place the pizza in the preheated oven and bake for 12-15 minutes or until the crust is golden, and the toppings are heated through.

Garnish and Serve:
- Once out of the oven, garnish the Vegan Taco Pizza with fresh cilantro. Serve slices with avocado slices and dollops of vegan sour cream or salsa if desired.

Enjoy the delicious flavors of a vegan taco in pizza form! This Vegan Taco Pizza is loaded with plant-based protein, vibrant veggies, and a perfect blend of taco seasonings. Customize the toppings to your liking and have a fiesta in every bite!

Jackfruit Carnitas Pizza

Ingredients:

For the Pizza Dough:

- 1 pizza dough (store-bought or homemade)

For the Jackfruit Carnitas:

- 1 can (20 oz) young green jackfruit in water or brine, drained and shredded
- 1 tablespoon olive oil
- 1 small onion, finely chopped
- 3 cloves garlic, minced
- 1 teaspoon ground cumin
- 1 teaspoon smoked paprika
- 1/2 teaspoon chili powder
- 1/2 teaspoon dried oregano
- Salt and pepper to taste
- Juice of 1 lime

For the Pizza Sauce:

- 1/2 cup tomato sauce
- 1 teaspoon dried oregano
- 1/2 teaspoon garlic powder
- Salt and pepper to taste

Additional Toppings:

- 1 cup shredded vegan cheese (cheddar or Mexican blend)
- 1/2 cup sliced red onions
- 1/2 cup sliced bell peppers (any color)
- Sliced jalapeños (optional for heat)
- Fresh cilantro, chopped

For Garnish:

- Avocado slices
- Lime wedges

Instructions:

Preparing the Jackfruit Carnitas:

Shred Jackfruit:
- Drain the canned jackfruit and shred it using a fork or your hands. Remove any seeds or hard pieces.

Cook Jackfruit Carnitas:
- In a skillet, heat olive oil over medium heat. Add chopped onions and minced garlic. Sauté until the onions are translucent.

Add Jackfruit and Spices:
- Add the shredded jackfruit to the skillet. Season with ground cumin, smoked paprika, chili powder, dried oregano, salt, and pepper. Sauté for 8-10 minutes until the jackfruit is well-coated with the spices.

Finish with Lime Juice:
- Squeeze lime juice over the jackfruit, mix well, and cook for an additional 2-3 minutes. Set aside.

Making the Pizza Sauce:

Prepare Pizza Sauce:
- In a bowl, mix together tomato sauce, dried oregano, garlic powder, salt, and pepper.

Assembling the Jackfruit Carnitas Pizza:

Preheat Oven:
- Preheat your oven according to the pizza dough package instructions or to 425°F (220°C).

Roll Out Pizza Dough:
- Roll out the pizza dough on a floured surface to your desired thickness.

Spread Pizza Sauce:
- Spread a layer of the prepared pizza sauce over the pizza dough.

Add Jackfruit Carnitas and Toppings:
- Evenly distribute the prepared jackfruit carnitas over the pizza sauce. Top with shredded vegan cheese, sliced red onions, sliced bell peppers, and sliced jalapeños if desired.

Bake:
- Place the pizza in the preheated oven and bake for 12-15 minutes or until the crust is golden, and the toppings are heated through.

Garnish and Serve:
- Once out of the oven, garnish the Jackfruit Carnitas Pizza with fresh cilantro. Serve slices with avocado slices and lime wedges.

Enjoy the savory and flavorful Jackfruit Carnitas Pizza! This plant-based alternative to traditional carnitas adds a delicious twist to your pizza. Customize with your favorite toppings and savor the jackfruit's texture and taste.

Vegan Chipotle BBQ Chick'n Pizza

Ingredients:

For the Pizza Dough:

- 1 pizza dough (store-bought or homemade)

For the Vegan Chipotle BBQ Chick'n:

- 1 cup vegan chicken substitute (seitan, soy curls, or your favorite meat alternative)
- 2 tablespoons olive oil
- 1/2 cup red onion, thinly sliced
- 1/2 cup bell peppers, thinly sliced (any color)
- 2 cloves garlic, minced
- 1/4 cup barbecue sauce
- 1-2 tablespoons chipotle sauce (adjust to your spice preference)
- Salt and pepper to taste

For the Pizza Sauce:

- 1/2 cup tomato sauce
- 1 teaspoon dried oregano
- 1/2 teaspoon garlic powder
- Salt and pepper to taste

Additional Toppings:

- 1 cup vegan cheese (smoked gouda or a blend of your choice)
- 1/4 cup corn kernels (fresh, frozen, or canned)
- Fresh cilantro, chopped

For Garnish:

- Avocado slices
- Lime wedges

Instructions:

Preparing the Vegan Chipotle BBQ Chick'n:

    Cook Vegan Chick'n:

- Cook the vegan chicken substitute according to package instructions. If using seitan or soy curls, sauté them in a pan with olive oil until lightly browned. Set aside.

Sauté Vegetables:

- In the same pan, add a bit more olive oil if needed. Sauté the sliced red onion, bell peppers, and minced garlic until softened.

Add Chipotle BBQ Sauce:

- Add the barbecue sauce and chipotle sauce to the pan, mixing well with the sautéed vegetables and vegan chick'n. Season with salt and pepper. Cook for an additional 2-3 minutes until everything is well-coated and heated through. Set aside.

Making the Pizza Sauce:

Prepare Pizza Sauce:

- In a bowl, mix together tomato sauce, dried oregano, garlic powder, salt, and pepper.

Assembling the Vegan Chipotle BBQ Chick'n Pizza:

Preheat Oven:

- Preheat your oven according to the pizza dough package instructions or to 425°F (220°C).

Roll Out Pizza Dough:

- Roll out the pizza dough on a floured surface to your desired thickness.

Spread Pizza Sauce:

- Spread a layer of the prepared pizza sauce over the pizza dough.

Add Vegan Chipotle BBQ Chick'n and Toppings:

- Evenly distribute the prepared vegan chipotle BBQ chick'n mixture over the pizza sauce. Top with vegan cheese and sprinkle corn kernels over the pizza.

Bake:

- Place the pizza in the preheated oven and bake for 12-15 minutes or until the crust is golden, and the toppings are heated through.

Garnish and Serve:

- Once out of the oven, garnish the Vegan Chipotle BBQ Chick'n Pizza with fresh cilantro. Serve slices with avocado slices and lime wedges.

Enjoy the smoky and spicy flavors of this Vegan Chipotle BBQ Chick'n Pizza! The combination of chipotle sauce, barbecue sauce, and vegan chick'n creates a mouthwatering and satisfying pizza. Customize the toppings to your liking and enjoy a delicious plant-based meal.

Mushroom and Spinach Mexican Pizza

Ingredients:

For the Pizza Dough:

- 1 pizza dough (store-bought or homemade)

For the Mushroom and Spinach Topping:

- 2 cups mushrooms, sliced (button or cremini)
- 2 cups fresh spinach, chopped
- 1 tablespoon olive oil
- 1 small onion, finely chopped
- 2 cloves garlic, minced
- 1 teaspoon ground cumin
- 1 teaspoon chili powder
- Salt and pepper to taste

For the Pizza Sauce:

- 1/2 cup tomato sauce
- 1 teaspoon dried oregano
- 1/2 teaspoon garlic powder
- Salt and pepper to taste

Additional Toppings:

- 1 cup shredded Mexican blend cheese or your favorite vegan cheese
- 1/2 cup black beans, cooked and drained
- Sliced jalapeños (optional for heat)
- Sliced black olives
- Chopped tomatoes

For Garnish:

- Fresh cilantro, chopped
- Avocado slices
- Lime wedges

Instructions:

Preparing the Mushroom and Spinach Topping:

Sauté Vegetables:
- In a skillet, heat olive oil over medium heat. Add chopped onions and minced garlic. Sauté until the onions are translucent.

Cook Mushrooms and Spinach:
- Add sliced mushrooms to the skillet and cook until they release their moisture and become tender. Add chopped spinach and cook until wilted.

Seasoning:
- Season the mixture with ground cumin, chili powder, salt, and pepper. Stir well and cook for an additional 2-3 minutes. Set aside.

Making the Pizza Sauce:

Prepare Pizza Sauce:
- In a bowl, mix together tomato sauce, dried oregano, garlic powder, salt, and pepper.

Assembling the Mushroom and Spinach Mexican Pizza:

Preheat Oven:
- Preheat your oven according to the pizza dough package instructions or to 425°F (220°C).

Roll Out Pizza Dough:
- Roll out the pizza dough on a floured surface to your desired thickness.

Spread Pizza Sauce:
- Spread a layer of the prepared pizza sauce over the pizza dough.

Add Mushroom and Spinach Topping and Toppings:
- Evenly distribute the prepared mushroom and spinach mixture over the pizza sauce. Top with shredded Mexican blend cheese, black beans, sliced jalapeños (if using), sliced black olives, and chopped tomatoes.

Bake:
- Place the pizza in the preheated oven and bake for 12-15 minutes or until the crust is golden, and the toppings are heated through.

Garnish and Serve:
- Once out of the oven, garnish the Mushroom and Spinach Mexican Pizza with fresh cilantro. Serve slices with avocado slices and lime wedges.

Enjoy the delightful combination of mushrooms, spinach, and Mexican flavors in this tasty pizza! Customize the toppings to suit your taste, and savor a delicious and veggie-packed meal.

Seafood Sensations:

Ceviche Pizza

Ingredients:

For the Pizza Dough:

- 1 pizza dough (store-bought or homemade)

For the Ceviche Topping:

- 1/2 pound fresh white fish (tilapia, cod, or any white fish), diced into small pieces
- 1/2 pound shrimp, peeled, deveined, and chopped
- Juice of 4-5 limes
- Juice of 2 lemons
- 1 small red onion, finely diced
- 1 jalapeño, seeded and finely chopped
- 1 cup cherry tomatoes, halved
- 1/2 cup cucumber, finely diced
- 1/4 cup fresh cilantro, chopped
- Salt and pepper to taste

For the Pizza Sauce:

- 1/4 cup olive oil
- 2 cloves garlic, minced
- Salt and pepper to taste

Additional Toppings:

- Avocado slices
- Radish slices
- Microgreens or arugula for garnish

Instructions:

Preparing the Ceviche Topping:

   Prepare Ceviche Base:
   - In a bowl, combine diced fish, chopped shrimp, lime juice, lemon juice, red onion, jalapeño, cherry tomatoes, cucumber, cilantro, salt, and pepper. Mix

well to ensure the seafood is evenly coated. Cover and let it marinate in the refrigerator for at least 30 minutes.

Preparing the Pizza Sauce:

Garlic Infused Olive Oil:
- In a small saucepan, heat olive oil over low heat. Add minced garlic and cook for 1-2 minutes until the garlic is fragrant. Season with salt and pepper. Remove from heat and set aside.

Assembling the Ceviche Pizza:

Preheat Oven:
- Preheat your oven according to the pizza dough package instructions or to 425°F (220°C).

Roll Out Pizza Dough:
- Roll out the pizza dough on a floured surface to your desired thickness.

Brush with Garlic Olive Oil:
- Brush the rolled-out dough with the garlic-infused olive oil, covering the entire surface.

Add Ceviche Topping:
- Spoon the marinated ceviche mixture evenly over the pizza dough.

Bake:
- Place the pizza in the preheated oven and bake for 12-15 minutes or until the crust is golden and cooked through.

Garnish and Serve:
- Once out of the oven, garnish the Ceviche Pizza with avocado slices, radish slices, and microgreens or arugula.

Serve slices of this Ceviche Pizza immediately for a refreshing and vibrant experience that combines the best of ceviche and pizza flavors. The tangy and citrusy seafood topping pairs wonderfully with the garlic-infused crust and fresh garnishes. Enjoy this unique fusion dish!

Spicy Tuna Tostada Pizza

Ingredients:

For the Pizza Dough:

- 1 pizza dough (store-bought or homemade)

For the Spicy Tuna Tostada Topping:

- 1 can (5 oz) of tuna in water, drained
- 2 tablespoons mayonnaise
- 1 tablespoon Sriracha sauce (adjust according to spice preference)
- 1 teaspoon soy sauce
- 1 teaspoon sesame oil
- 2 green onions, finely chopped
- 1/4 cup cucumber, finely diced
- 1/4 cup radishes, thinly sliced
- 1 tablespoon cilantro, chopped
- Sesame seeds for garnish (optional)

For the Pizza Sauce:

- 1/4 cup soy sauce
- 1 tablespoon rice vinegar
- 1 tablespoon honey or agave syrup
- 1 teaspoon sesame oil
- 1 teaspoon grated ginger
- 1 clove garlic, minced

Additional Toppings:

- 1/2 cup shredded lettuce
- 1/4 cup shredded carrots
- Avocado slices

Instructions:

Preparing the Spicy Tuna Tostada Topping:

Prepare Tuna Mixture:

- In a bowl, combine drained tuna, mayonnaise, Sriracha sauce, soy sauce, sesame oil, green onions, diced cucumber, radishes, and chopped cilantro. Mix well until all ingredients are evenly coated.

Preparing the Pizza Sauce:

Prepare Soy-Ginger Sauce:
- In a small bowl, whisk together soy sauce, rice vinegar, honey or agave syrup, sesame oil, grated ginger, and minced garlic. Set aside.

Assembling the Spicy Tuna Tostada Pizza:

Preheat Oven:
- Preheat your oven according to the pizza dough package instructions or to 425°F (220°C).

Roll Out Pizza Dough:
- Roll out the pizza dough on a floured surface to your desired thickness.

Spread Soy-Ginger Sauce:
- Spread a layer of the prepared soy-ginger sauce over the pizza dough.

Add Spicy Tuna Tostada Topping:
- Spoon the spicy tuna tostada mixture evenly over the pizza sauce.

Bake:
- Place the pizza in the preheated oven and bake for 12-15 minutes or until the crust is golden and cooked through.

Garnish and Serve:
- Once out of the oven, garnish the Spicy Tuna Tostada Pizza with shredded lettuce, shredded carrots, and avocado slices. Sprinkle sesame seeds on top if desired.

Serve slices of this Spicy Tuna Tostada Pizza for a fusion of Japanese and Mexican flavors. The spicy tuna mixture on a pizza crust provides a unique and delicious twist. Customize with your favorite toppings and enjoy a delightful meal!

Seafood Enchilada Pizza

Ingredients:

For the Pizza Dough:

- 1 pizza dough (store-bought or homemade)

For the Seafood Enchilada Topping:

- 1/2 pound shrimp, peeled, deveined, and chopped
- 1/2 pound scallops, chopped
- 1 tablespoon olive oil
- 1 small onion, finely chopped
- 2 cloves garlic, minced
- 1 teaspoon ground cumin
- 1 teaspoon chili powder
- 1/2 teaspoon smoked paprika
- Salt and pepper to taste
- 1 cup enchilada sauce (store-bought or homemade)

For the Pizza Sauce:

- 1/2 cup tomato sauce
- 1 teaspoon dried oregano
- 1/2 teaspoon garlic powder
- Salt and pepper to taste

Additional Toppings:

- 1 cup shredded Mexican blend cheese
- Sliced jalapeños (optional for heat)
- Sliced black olives
- Chopped green onions
- Fresh cilantro, chopped

Instructions:

Preparing the Seafood Enchilada Topping:

Cook Seafood:

- In a skillet, heat olive oil over medium heat. Add chopped onions and minced garlic. Sauté until the onions are translucent.

Add Shrimp and Scallops:
- Add chopped shrimp and scallops to the skillet. Season with ground cumin, chili powder, smoked paprika, salt, and pepper. Cook for 4-5 minutes until the seafood is cooked through.

Enchilada Sauce:
- Pour enchilada sauce over the cooked seafood mixture. Stir well to combine and let it simmer for an additional 2-3 minutes. Set aside.

Making the Pizza Sauce:

Prepare Pizza Sauce:
- In a bowl, mix together tomato sauce, dried oregano, garlic powder, salt, and pepper.

Assembling the Seafood Enchilada Pizza:

Preheat Oven:
- Preheat your oven according to the pizza dough package instructions or to 425°F (220°C).

Roll Out Pizza Dough:
- Roll out the pizza dough on a floured surface to your desired thickness.

Spread Pizza Sauce:
- Spread a layer of the prepared pizza sauce over the pizza dough.

Add Seafood Enchilada Topping and Toppings:
- Spoon the prepared seafood enchilada mixture evenly over the pizza sauce. Top with shredded Mexican blend cheese, sliced jalapeños (if using), sliced black olives, chopped green onions, and fresh cilantro.

Bake:
- Place the pizza in the preheated oven and bake for 12-15 minutes or until the crust is golden, and the toppings are heated through.

Garnish and Serve:
- Once out of the oven, garnish the Seafood Enchilada Pizza with additional cilantro. Slice and serve hot.

Enjoy the delicious flavors of seafood enchiladas in pizza form! This fusion dish brings together the best of both worlds with a seafood-rich topping and the convenience of a pizza. Customize with your preferred toppings and savor a delightful meal.

Grilled Fish Taco Pizza

Ingredients:

For the Pizza Dough:

- 1 pizza dough (store-bought or homemade)

For the Grilled Fish Taco Topping:

- 1 pound white fish fillets (tilapia, cod, or your choice)
- 2 tablespoons olive oil
- Juice of 2 limes
- 1 teaspoon ground cumin
- 1 teaspoon chili powder
- 1/2 teaspoon smoked paprika
- Salt and pepper to taste

For the Pizza Sauce:

- 1/4 cup sour cream or Greek yogurt
- 1 tablespoon mayonnaise
- 1 tablespoon lime juice
- 1 teaspoon taco seasoning

Additional Toppings:

- 1 cup shredded lettuce
- 1 cup cherry tomatoes, halved
- 1/2 cup red onion, thinly sliced
- 1/2 cup sliced black olives
- 1/4 cup fresh cilantro, chopped
- Sliced jalapeños (optional for heat)

For Garnish:

- Avocado slices
- Lime wedges

Instructions:

Preparing the Grilled Fish Taco Topping:

Marinate Fish:
- In a bowl, combine olive oil, lime juice, ground cumin, chili powder, smoked paprika, salt, and pepper. Marinate the fish fillets in this mixture for at least 30 minutes.

Grill Fish:
- Preheat the grill or grill pan. Grill the marinated fish fillets for 3-4 minutes per side or until cooked through. Once cooked, flake the fish into bite-sized pieces. Set aside.

Making the Pizza Sauce:

Prepare Taco Sauce:
- In a small bowl, mix together sour cream or Greek yogurt, mayonnaise, lime juice, and taco seasoning. Set aside.

Assembling the Grilled Fish Taco Pizza:

Preheat Oven:
- Preheat your oven according to the pizza dough package instructions or to 425°F (220°C).

Roll Out Pizza Dough:
- Roll out the pizza dough on a floured surface to your desired thickness.

Spread Taco Sauce:
- Spread a layer of the prepared taco sauce over the pizza dough.

Add Grilled Fish Taco Topping and Toppings:
- Evenly distribute the grilled fish over the taco sauce. Top with shredded lettuce, cherry tomatoes, sliced red onion, black olives, chopped cilantro, and sliced jalapeños if desired.

Bake:
- Place the pizza in the preheated oven and bake for 12-15 minutes or until the crust is golden, and the toppings are heated through.

Garnish and Serve:
- Once out of the oven, garnish the Grilled Fish Taco Pizza with avocado slices. Serve slices with lime wedges.

Enjoy the flavors of grilled fish tacos in pizza form! This fusion dish combines the elements of a classic fish taco with the convenience of pizza. Customize with your favorite toppings and savor a delicious meal that's perfect for a summer barbecue or weeknight dinner.

Shrimp Diablo Pizza

Ingredients:

For the Pizza Dough:

- 1 pizza dough (store-bought or homemade)

For the Shrimp Diablo Topping:

- 1 pound large shrimp, peeled and deveined
- 2 tablespoons olive oil
- 3 cloves garlic, minced
- 1 teaspoon red pepper flakes (adjust to your spice preference)
- 1 can (14 oz) diced tomatoes, drained
- 1 teaspoon dried oregano
- Salt and pepper to taste

For the Pizza Sauce:

- 1/4 cup tomato sauce
- 1 teaspoon dried basil
- 1/2 teaspoon garlic powder
- Salt and pepper to taste

Additional Toppings:

- 1 cup shredded mozzarella cheese
- 1/4 cup grated Parmesan cheese
- Fresh basil leaves for garnish

Instructions:

Preparing the Shrimp Diablo Topping:

Sauté Shrimp:
- In a skillet, heat olive oil over medium heat. Add minced garlic and red pepper flakes. Sauté for 1-2 minutes until the garlic is fragrant.

Cook Shrimp:
- Add the peeled and deveined shrimp to the skillet. Cook until the shrimp turn pink and opaque, about 2-3 minutes.

Add Tomatoes:

- Add diced tomatoes, dried oregano, salt, and pepper to the skillet. Cook for an additional 2-3 minutes until the mixture is well combined and heated through. Set aside.

Making the Pizza Sauce:

Prepare Pizza Sauce:
- In a bowl, mix together tomato sauce, dried basil, garlic powder, salt, and pepper.

Assembling the Shrimp Diablo Pizza:

Preheat Oven:
- Preheat your oven according to the pizza dough package instructions or to 425°F (220°C).

Roll Out Pizza Dough:
- Roll out the pizza dough on a floured surface to your desired thickness.

Spread Pizza Sauce:
- Spread a layer of the prepared pizza sauce over the pizza dough.

Add Shrimp Diablo Topping and Toppings:
- Spoon the prepared shrimp diablo mixture evenly over the pizza sauce. Top with shredded mozzarella cheese and grated Parmesan cheese.

Bake:
- Place the pizza in the preheated oven and bake for 12-15 minutes or until the crust is golden, and the toppings are bubbly and slightly browned.

Garnish and Serve:
- Once out of the oven, garnish the Shrimp Diablo Pizza with fresh basil leaves. Slice and serve hot.

Enjoy the bold and spicy flavors of Shrimp Diablo on a delicious pizza crust! This pizza is perfect for those who love a bit of heat and seafood. Customize with additional toppings if desired and savor a delightful and zesty meal.

Crab and Avocado Pizza

Ingredients:

For the Pizza Dough:

- 1 pizza dough (store-bought or homemade)

For the Crab and Avocado Topping:

- 1 cup lump crab meat, picked over for shells
- 1 avocado, sliced
- 1 tablespoon olive oil
- 2 cloves garlic, minced
- Juice of 1 lemon
- Salt and pepper to taste
- Red pepper flakes for a hint of spice (optional)

For the Pizza Sauce:

- 1/4 cup mayonnaise
- 1 tablespoon Dijon mustard
- 1 tablespoon lemon juice
- 1 clove garlic, minced
- Salt and pepper to taste

Additional Toppings:

- 1 cup shredded mozzarella cheese
- 1/4 cup grated Parmesan cheese
- Fresh chives, chopped, for garnish

Instructions:

Preparing the Crab and Avocado Topping:

Prepare Crab and Avocado Mixture:
- In a bowl, gently combine lump crab meat, sliced avocado, olive oil, minced garlic, lemon juice, salt, pepper, and red pepper flakes if using. Be careful not to break up the crab meat too much. Set aside.

Making the Pizza Sauce:

Prepare Mayo-Mustard Sauce:
- In a bowl, mix together mayonnaise, Dijon mustard, lemon juice, minced garlic, salt, and pepper.

Assembling the Crab and Avocado Pizza:

Preheat Oven:
- Preheat your oven according to the pizza dough package instructions or to 425°F (220°C).

Roll Out Pizza Dough:
- Roll out the pizza dough on a floured surface to your desired thickness.

Spread Pizza Sauce:
- Spread a layer of the prepared mayo-mustard sauce over the pizza dough.

Add Crab and Avocado Topping and Toppings:
- Spoon the crab and avocado mixture evenly over the pizza sauce. Top with shredded mozzarella cheese and grated Parmesan cheese.

Bake:
- Place the pizza in the preheated oven and bake for 12-15 minutes or until the crust is golden, and the toppings are bubbly and slightly browned.

Garnish and Serve:
- Once out of the oven, garnish the Crab and Avocado Pizza with fresh chives. Slice and serve hot.

Enjoy the combination of succulent crab meat and creamy avocado on a delightful pizza crust! This pizza is a perfect blend of flavors, and the mayo-mustard sauce adds a zesty kick. Customize with additional toppings or herbs if desired, and savor a delicious and unique seafood pizza.

Lobster and Mango Salsa Pizza

Ingredients:

For the Pizza Dough:

- 1 pizza dough (store-bought or homemade)

For the Lobster and Mango Salsa Topping:

- 1 1/2 cups cooked lobster meat, chopped
- 1 mango, peeled, pitted, and diced
- 1/2 red onion, finely chopped
- 1/4 cup fresh cilantro, chopped
- Juice of 1 lime
- Salt and pepper to taste
- Red pepper flakes for a hint of spice (optional)

For the Pizza Sauce:

- 1/4 cup garlic-infused olive oil
- Salt and pepper to taste

Additional Toppings:

- 1 cup shredded mozzarella cheese
- 1/4 cup crumbled feta cheese
- Arugula for garnish

Instructions:

Preparing the Lobster and Mango Salsa Topping:

Prepare Lobster and Mango Salsa:
- In a bowl, combine chopped lobster meat, diced mango, finely chopped red onion, chopped cilantro, lime juice, salt, pepper, and red pepper flakes if using. Mix well and set aside.

Making the Pizza Sauce:

Prepare Garlic-Infused Olive Oil:
- In a small bowl, mix together olive oil, minced garlic, salt, and pepper.

Assembling the Lobster and Mango Salsa Pizza:

Preheat Oven:
- Preheat your oven according to the pizza dough package instructions or to 425°F (220°C).

Roll Out Pizza Dough:
- Roll out the pizza dough on a floured surface to your desired thickness.

Spread Garlic-Infused Olive Oil:
- Spread a layer of the prepared garlic-infused olive oil over the pizza dough.

Add Lobster and Mango Salsa Topping and Toppings:
- Spoon the lobster and mango salsa mixture evenly over the pizza dough. Top with shredded mozzarella cheese and crumbled feta cheese.

Bake:
- Place the pizza in the preheated oven and bake for 12-15 minutes or until the crust is golden, and the toppings are bubbly and slightly browned.

Garnish and Serve:
- Once out of the oven, garnish the Lobster and Mango Salsa Pizza with fresh arugula. Slice and serve hot.

Enjoy the luxurious combination of lobster and sweet mango salsa on a delicious pizza crust! The garlic-infused olive oil adds a rich flavor, and the combination of cheeses complements the toppings perfectly. Customize with additional herbs or spices if desired and savor this unique and tasty seafood pizza.

Chipotle Lime Salmon Pizza

Ingredients:

For the Pizza Dough:

- 1 pizza dough (store-bought or homemade)

For the Chipotle Lime Salmon Topping:

- 1 pound salmon fillet, skin removed
- 2 tablespoons olive oil
- Zest and juice of 1 lime
- 2 teaspoons chipotle powder
- 1 teaspoon ground cumin
- 1 teaspoon garlic powder
- Salt and pepper to taste

For the Pizza Sauce:

- 1/4 cup sour cream
- 1 tablespoon adobo sauce (from a can of chipotle peppers in adobo)
- 1 tablespoon lime juice
- Salt and pepper to taste

Additional Toppings:

- 1 cup shredded pepper jack cheese
- 1/2 cup red onion, thinly sliced
- 1/4 cup fresh cilantro, chopped
- Sliced jalapeños for extra heat (optional)

Instructions:

Preparing the Chipotle Lime Salmon Topping:

Preheat Oven:
- Preheat your oven according to the pizza dough package instructions or to 425°F (220°C).

Marinate Salmon:

- In a bowl, mix together olive oil, lime zest, lime juice, chipotle powder, ground cumin, garlic powder, salt, and pepper. Place the salmon fillet in the marinade and let it marinate for at least 15 minutes.

Cook Salmon:
- Heat a skillet over medium-high heat. Add the marinated salmon and cook for 3-4 minutes per side or until the salmon is cooked through. Flake the salmon into bite-sized pieces.

Making the Pizza Sauce:

Prepare Chipotle Lime Sauce:
- In a bowl, combine sour cream, adobo sauce, lime juice, salt, and pepper. Mix well to create the chipotle lime sauce.

Assembling the Chipotle Lime Salmon Pizza:

Roll Out Pizza Dough:
- Roll out the pizza dough on a floured surface to your desired thickness.

Spread Chipotle Lime Sauce:
- Spread a layer of the prepared chipotle lime sauce over the pizza dough.

Add Chipotle Lime Salmon Topping and Toppings:
- Sprinkle the flaked chipotle lime salmon evenly over the pizza. Top with shredded pepper jack cheese, thinly sliced red onion, and chopped cilantro. Add sliced jalapeños if you desire extra heat.

Bake:
- Place the pizza in the preheated oven and bake for 12-15 minutes or until the crust is golden, and the toppings are bubbly and slightly browned.

Garnish and Serve:
- Once out of the oven, garnish the Chipotle Lime Salmon Pizza with additional cilantro. Slice and serve hot.

Enjoy the bold and smoky flavors of chipotle lime salmon on a tasty pizza crust! The chipotle lime sauce adds a zesty kick, and the combination of cheeses and toppings creates a delicious balance. Customize with your favorite additions and savor a unique and flavorful salmon pizza.

Tuna Melt Quesadilla Pizza

Ingredients:

For the Quesadilla Pizza:

- 2 large flour tortillas
- 1 cup shredded cheddar cheese
- 1 cup shredded mozzarella cheese

For the Tuna Melt Topping:

- 1 can (5 oz) tuna, drained
- 1/4 cup mayonnaise
- 2 tablespoons diced red onion
- 1 tablespoon chopped fresh parsley
- 1 teaspoon Dijon mustard
- Salt and pepper to taste

Additional Toppings:

- 1/4 cup sliced black olives
- 1/4 cup diced tomatoes
- 2 tablespoons chopped green onions

Instructions:

Preparing the Tuna Melt Topping:

Prepare Tuna Mixture:
- In a bowl, combine drained tuna, mayonnaise, diced red onion, chopped parsley, Dijon mustard, salt, and pepper. Mix well until all ingredients are evenly combined. Set aside.

Assembling the Tuna Melt Quesadilla Pizza:

Preheat Oven:
- Preheat your oven to 425°F (220°C).

Assemble Quesadilla Pizza:
- Place one flour tortilla on a baking sheet. Sprinkle a layer of shredded cheddar cheese and mozzarella cheese over the tortilla. Add a second tortilla on top.

Bake Quesadilla:

- Bake in the preheated oven for about 8-10 minutes or until the cheese is melted, and the edges are golden.

Add Tuna Melt Topping:
- Remove the quesadilla from the oven. Spread the prepared tuna melt mixture over the top of the quesadilla.

Add Additional Toppings:
- Sprinkle sliced black olives, diced tomatoes, and chopped green onions over the tuna melt topping.

Broil:
- Turn on the broiler and place the baking sheet back in the oven. Broil for 2-3 minutes or until the topping is heated through and slightly bubbly.

Garnish and Serve:
- Once out of the oven, garnish with additional chopped parsley or green onions if desired. Slice into wedges and serve hot.

Enjoy the flavors of a tuna melt on a crispy quesadilla crust! This recipe combines the comfort of a tuna melt with the convenience and crunch of a quesadilla. Customize with your favorite toppings and herbs for added freshness.

Squid Ink Seafood Pizza

Ingredients:

For the Squid Ink Pizza Dough:

- 1 pizza dough ball (store-bought or homemade)
- 2 teaspoons squid ink

For the Squid Ink Aioli Sauce:

- 1/2 cup mayonnaise
- 1 teaspoon squid ink
- 1 clove garlic, minced
- 1 tablespoon lemon juice
- Salt and pepper to taste

For the Seafood Topping:

- 1/2 cup squid rings and tentacles, cleaned
- 1/2 cup shrimp, peeled and deveined
- 1/2 cup scallops
- 2 tablespoons olive oil
- 2 cloves garlic, minced
- Salt and pepper to taste
- Zest of 1 lemon

Additional Toppings:

- 1/2 cup cherry tomatoes, halved
- Fresh basil leaves for garnish

Instructions:

Preparing the Squid Ink Pizza Dough:

Incorporate Squid Ink:
- Knead the squid ink into the pizza dough until it's evenly distributed and the dough takes on a consistent color.

Roll Out Dough:
- Roll out the squid ink-infused pizza dough on a floured surface to your desired thickness.

Making the Squid Ink Aioli Sauce:

Prepare Squid Ink Aioli:
- In a bowl, mix together mayonnaise, squid ink, minced garlic, lemon juice, salt, and pepper. Adjust the seasoning to your liking. Set aside.

Preparing the Seafood Topping:

Cook Seafood:
- In a skillet, heat olive oil over medium heat. Add minced garlic and cook until fragrant. Add squid rings, tentacles, shrimp, and scallops. Cook for 3-4 minutes until the seafood is just cooked through. Season with salt and pepper. Add lemon zest and toss to combine. Remove from heat.

Assembling the Squid Ink Seafood Pizza:

Preheat Oven:
- Preheat your oven according to the pizza dough package instructions or to 425°F (220°C).

Spread Squid Ink Aioli:
- Spread a layer of the prepared squid ink aioli sauce over the rolled-out pizza dough.

Add Seafood Topping and Additional Toppings:
- Distribute the cooked seafood evenly over the aioli-covered pizza dough. Scatter halved cherry tomatoes on top.

Bake:
- Place the pizza in the preheated oven and bake for 12-15 minutes or until the crust is golden, and the toppings are heated through.

Garnish and Serve:
- Once out of the oven, garnish the Squid Ink Seafood Pizza with fresh basil leaves. Slice and serve hot.

Enjoy the bold and briny flavors of squid ink and seafood on this unique pizza! The combination of squid ink-infused dough, flavorful aioli, and a medley of fresh seafood creates a deliciously distinctive dish. Customize with your preferred toppings and savor this gourmet seafood pizza.

Sweet Dessert Pizzas:

Churro Dessert Pizza

Ingredients:

For the Pizza Dough:

- 1 pizza dough (store-bought or homemade)

For the Churro Topping:

- 1/2 cup unsalted butter
- 1 cup water
- 2 tablespoons granulated sugar
- 1 cup all-purpose flour
- 1/4 teaspoon salt
- 3 large eggs
- Vegetable oil for frying

For the Cinnamon Sugar Coating:

- 1/2 cup granulated sugar
- 2 teaspoons ground cinnamon

For the Cream Cheese Drizzle:

- 4 oz cream cheese, softened
- 1/2 cup powdered sugar
- 1 teaspoon vanilla extract
- 2-3 tablespoons milk

Additional Toppings:

- Sliced strawberries, bananas, or other fruits (optional)
- Whipped cream (optional)
- Chocolate sauce (optional)

Instructions:

Preparing the Churro Topping:

Make Churro Dough:
- In a saucepan, combine butter, water, and granulated sugar. Bring to a boil. Remove from heat and stir in flour and salt until well combined.

Add Eggs:
- Allow the mixture to cool slightly. Then, beat in the eggs one at a time until smooth and well incorporated.

Fry Churros:
- Heat vegetable oil in a deep fryer or a heavy-bottomed pot to 375°F (190°C). Spoon the churro dough into a piping bag fitted with a star tip. Pipe strips of dough into the hot oil, cutting with scissors. Fry until golden brown, then transfer to a paper towel-lined plate.

Coat with Cinnamon Sugar:
- In a bowl, combine granulated sugar and ground cinnamon. Roll the fried churros in the cinnamon sugar mixture until well coated.

Making the Cream Cheese Drizzle:

Prepare Cream Cheese Drizzle:
- In a bowl, beat together softened cream cheese, powdered sugar, vanilla extract, and milk until smooth and creamy. Adjust the consistency by adding more milk if needed.

Assembling the Churro Dessert Pizza:

Preheat Oven:
- Preheat your oven according to the pizza dough package instructions or to 425°F (220°C).

Roll Out Pizza Dough:
- Roll out the pizza dough on a floured surface to your desired thickness.

Bake:
- Place the pizza dough on a baking sheet. Bake in the preheated oven until the crust is golden, following the instructions on the pizza dough package.

Arrange Churros:
- Arrange the cinnamon sugar-coated churros on top of the baked pizza crust.

Drizzle Cream Cheese Sauce:
- Drizzle the cream cheese sauce over the churros.

Add Additional Toppings:
- Optionally, add sliced strawberries, bananas, or other fruits. Finish with whipped cream and a drizzle of chocolate sauce if desired.

Slice and Serve:
- Slice the Churro Dessert Pizza into portions and serve warm.

Enjoy the sweet and cinnamony goodness of a Churro Dessert Pizza! This delightful treat combines the flavors of churros with a pizza twist. Customize with your favorite toppings and indulge in a delicious dessert experience.

Mexican Chocolate Dessert Pizza

Ingredients:

For the Pizza Dough:

- 1 pizza dough (store-bought or homemade)

For the Mexican Chocolate Sauce:

- 1/2 cup heavy cream
- 1 cup semisweet chocolate chips
- 1 tablespoon unsweetened cocoa powder
- 1 teaspoon ground cinnamon
- 1/2 teaspoon chili powder (adjust to taste)
- 1/4 teaspoon cayenne pepper (optional, for extra heat)
- Pinch of salt

For the Toppings:

- 1/2 cup sliced strawberries
- 1/4 cup chopped toasted almonds
- Powdered sugar for dusting
- Vanilla ice cream (optional, for serving)

Instructions:

Preparing the Mexican Chocolate Sauce:

Make Chocolate Sauce:
- In a saucepan, heat the heavy cream until it starts to simmer (but not boil). Remove from heat and add chocolate chips, cocoa powder, ground cinnamon, chili powder, cayenne pepper (if using), and a pinch of salt. Stir until the chocolate is fully melted and the sauce is smooth. Set aside to cool.

Assembling the Mexican Chocolate Dessert Pizza:

Preheat Oven:
- Preheat your oven according to the pizza dough package instructions or to 425°F (220°C).

Roll Out Pizza Dough:
- Roll out the pizza dough on a floured surface to your desired thickness.

Bake:

- Place the pizza dough on a baking sheet. Bake in the preheated oven until the crust is golden, following the instructions on the pizza dough package.

Spread Chocolate Sauce:
- Once the pizza crust is baked, spread the Mexican chocolate sauce evenly over the crust.

Add Toppings:
- Sprinkle sliced strawberries and chopped toasted almonds over the chocolate sauce.

Optional: Broil for a Minute:
- Optionally, you can place the pizza under the broiler for about a minute to slightly melt the toppings and enhance the flavors.

Dust with Powdered Sugar:
- Dust the Mexican Chocolate Dessert Pizza with powdered sugar for a finishing touch.

Serve with Ice Cream:
- Optionally, serve slices of the dessert pizza with a scoop of vanilla ice cream for an extra indulgence.

Slice and Serve:
- Slice the Mexican Chocolate Dessert Pizza into portions and serve warm.

Enjoy the rich and spicy flavors of Mexican chocolate in this dessert pizza! The combination of chocolate, cinnamon, and a hint of chili creates a unique and indulgent treat. Customize with your favorite toppings and savor the deliciousness of this delightful dessert.

Dulce de Leche Banana Pizza

Ingredients:

For the Pizza Dough:

- 1 pizza dough (store-bought or homemade)

For the Dulce de Leche Sauce:

- 1 cup dulce de leche (store-bought or homemade)

For the Toppings:

- 2 ripe bananas, sliced
- 1/2 cup chopped walnuts or pecans
- 1/4 cup shredded coconut
- 1/4 cup chocolate chips or chocolate chunks
- Powdered sugar for dusting (optional)

Instructions:

Assembling the Dulce de Leche Banana Pizza:

Preheat Oven:
- Preheat your oven according to the pizza dough package instructions or to 425°F (220°C).

Roll Out Pizza Dough:
- Roll out the pizza dough on a floured surface to your desired thickness.

Bake:
- Place the pizza dough on a baking sheet. Bake in the preheated oven until the crust is golden, following the instructions on the pizza dough package.

Spread Dulce de Leche:
- Once the pizza crust is baked, spread the dulce de leche sauce evenly over the crust.

Add Banana Slices and Toppings:
- Arrange the sliced bananas over the dulce de leche-covered crust. Sprinkle chopped nuts, shredded coconut, and chocolate chips or chunks on top.

Optional: Broil for a Minute:
- Optionally, you can place the pizza under the broiler for about a minute to slightly melt the toppings and enhance the flavors.

Dust with Powdered Sugar:
- Optionally, dust the Dulce de Leche Banana Pizza with powdered sugar for a finishing touch.

Slice and Serve:
- Slice the pizza into portions and serve warm.

Enjoy the delightful combination of sweet dulce de leche, creamy bananas, and a variety of toppings on this dessert pizza! Customize with your favorite nuts or additional toppings as desired. This pizza is perfect for satisfying your sweet tooth with a Latin American twist.

Tres Leches Fruit Pizza

Ingredients:

For the Pizza Dough:

- 1 pizza dough (store-bought or homemade)

For the Tres Leches Sauce:

- 1 can (14 ounces) sweetened condensed milk
- 1 can (12 ounces) evaporated milk
- 1 cup whole milk
- 1 teaspoon vanilla extract

For the Toppings:

- 2 cups whipped cream
- Assorted fresh fruits (strawberries, kiwi, mango, etc.), sliced
- Shredded coconut (optional)
- Mint leaves for garnish (optional)

Instructions:

Assembling the Tres Leches Fruit Pizza:

Preheat Oven:
- Preheat your oven according to the pizza dough package instructions or to 425°F (220°C).

Roll Out Pizza Dough:
- Roll out the pizza dough on a floured surface to your desired thickness.

Bake:
- Place the pizza dough on a baking sheet. Bake in the preheated oven until the crust is golden, following the instructions on the pizza dough package.

Prepare Tres Leches Sauce:
- In a bowl, whisk together sweetened condensed milk, evaporated milk, whole milk, and vanilla extract to create the tres leches sauce.

Poke Holes in the Pizza:
- Once the pizza crust is baked, use a fork to poke holes all over the surface. This will allow the tres leches sauce to be absorbed.

Pour Tres Leches Sauce:

- Pour the tres leches sauce evenly over the baked pizza crust. Allow it to soak in for a few minutes.

Spread Whipped Cream:
- Spread a layer of whipped cream over the tres leches-soaked crust.

Add Sliced Fruits:
- Arrange the sliced fresh fruits on top of the whipped cream. You can use a variety of fruits for a colorful and vibrant appearance.

Optional: Sprinkle Coconut and Garnish:
- Optionally, sprinkle shredded coconut over the pizza for added texture. Garnish with mint leaves for a fresh touch.

Chill Before Serving:
- Refrigerate the Tres Leches Fruit Pizza for at least 2-3 hours to allow the flavors to meld and the dessert to set.

Slice and Serve:
- Slice the pizza into portions and serve chilled.

Enjoy this delightful Tres Leches Fruit Pizza, combining the richness of tres leches with the freshness of assorted fruits! It's a sweet and refreshing dessert that's perfect for any occasion.

Mango Coconut Dessert Pizza

Ingredients:

For the Pizza Dough:

- 1 pizza dough (store-bought or homemade)

For the Coconut Cream Sauce:

- 1 can (14 ounces) coconut milk
- 1/4 cup sweetened condensed milk
- 1/2 teaspoon vanilla extract

For the Toppings:

- 2 ripe mangoes, peeled, pitted, and thinly sliced
- 1/2 cup shredded coconut, toasted
- 1/4 cup chopped macadamia nuts, toasted
- Honey for drizzling
- Mint leaves for garnish (optional)

Instructions:

Assembling the Mango Coconut Dessert Pizza:

Preheat Oven:
- Preheat your oven according to the pizza dough package instructions or to 425°F (220°C).

Roll Out Pizza Dough:
- Roll out the pizza dough on a floured surface to your desired thickness.

Bake:
- Place the pizza dough on a baking sheet. Bake in the preheated oven until the crust is golden, following the instructions on the pizza dough package.

Prepare Coconut Cream Sauce:
- In a saucepan, heat coconut milk over medium heat. Stir in sweetened condensed milk and vanilla extract. Simmer for a few minutes until well combined. Remove from heat and let it cool.

Spread Coconut Cream Sauce:
- Once the pizza crust is baked, spread the coconut cream sauce evenly over the crust.

Add Mango Slices:
- Arrange the thinly sliced mangoes over the coconut cream sauce.

Sprinkle with Toasted Coconut and Macadamia Nuts:
- Sprinkle toasted shredded coconut and chopped toasted macadamia nuts over the mango slices.

Optional: Drizzle with Honey:
- Drizzle honey over the top for added sweetness.

Optional: Garnish with Mint Leaves:
- Optionally, garnish the Mango Coconut Dessert Pizza with fresh mint leaves for a pop of color and freshness.

Slice and Serve:
- Slice the pizza into portions and serve immediately.

Enjoy the tropical flavors of mango and coconut in this delightful dessert pizza! The combination of creamy coconut sauce, sweet mango slices, and crunchy toasted toppings creates a heavenly treat. Customize with additional fruits or toppings according to your preference.

Pineapple and Rum Raisin Dessert Pizza

Ingredients:

For the Pizza Dough:

- 1 pizza dough (store-bought or homemade)

For the Rum Raisin Sauce:

- 1/2 cup raisins
- 1/4 cup dark rum
- 1/4 cup water
- 2 tablespoons brown sugar

For the Pineapple Topping:

- 1 cup fresh pineapple chunks
- 2 tablespoons brown sugar
- 1 tablespoon unsalted butter

For the Cream Cheese Drizzle:

- 4 oz cream cheese, softened
- 1/4 cup powdered sugar
- 1 teaspoon vanilla extract
- 2-3 tablespoons milk

For Garnish:

- 1/4 cup chopped walnuts or pecans (optional)

Instructions:

Preparing the Rum Raisin Sauce:

Prepare Rum Raisin Mixture:
- In a small saucepan, combine raisins, dark rum, water, and brown sugar. Bring to a simmer over medium heat. Let it simmer for about 5 minutes until the raisins are plump and the liquid is slightly reduced. Remove from heat and set aside.

Preparing the Pineapple Topping:

Caramelize Pineapple:

- In a skillet, melt butter over medium heat. Add pineapple chunks and brown sugar. Cook for 3-4 minutes, stirring occasionally, until the pineapple is caramelized. Remove from heat and set aside.

Making the Cream Cheese Drizzle:

Prepare Cream Cheese Drizzle:
- In a bowl, beat together softened cream cheese, powdered sugar, vanilla extract, and milk until smooth and creamy. Adjust the consistency by adding more milk if needed.

Assembling the Pineapple and Rum Raisin Dessert Pizza:

Preheat Oven:
- Preheat your oven according to the pizza dough package instructions or to 425°F (220°C).

Roll Out Pizza Dough:
- Roll out the pizza dough on a floured surface to your desired thickness.

Bake:
- Place the pizza dough on a baking sheet. Bake in the preheated oven until the crust is golden, following the instructions on the pizza dough package.

Spread Rum Raisin Sauce:
- Once the pizza crust is baked, spread the rum raisin sauce evenly over the crust.

Add Caramelized Pineapple:
- Arrange the caramelized pineapple chunks over the rum raisin sauce.

Drizzle with Cream Cheese Sauce:
- Drizzle the cream cheese sauce over the pineapple.

Optional: Garnish with Chopped Nuts:
- Optionally, sprinkle chopped walnuts or pecans over the top for added crunch.

Slice and Serve:
- Slice the Pineapple and Rum Raisin Dessert Pizza into portions and serve warm.

Enjoy the tropical sweetness of pineapple, the rich flavor of rum-infused raisins, and the creamy touch of the cream cheese drizzle in this delightful dessert pizza! Customize with your favorite nuts or additional toppings as desired.

Avocado Lime Dessert Pizza

Ingredients:

For the Pizza Dough:

- 1 pizza dough (store-bought or homemade)

For the Avocado Lime Cream:

- 2 ripe avocados, peeled and pitted
- 1/4 cup condensed milk
- Zest and juice of 2 limes
- 2 tablespoons honey (adjust to taste)

For the Toppings:

- Sliced kiwi
- Sliced strawberries
- Sliced bananas
- Fresh mint leaves for garnish

Instructions:

Making the Avocado Lime Cream:

Prepare Avocado Lime Cream:
- In a blender or food processor, combine ripe avocados, condensed milk, lime zest, lime juice, and honey. Blend until smooth and creamy. Adjust sweetness with more honey if needed. Set aside.

Assembling the Avocado Lime Dessert Pizza:

Preheat Oven:
- Preheat your oven according to the pizza dough package instructions or to 425°F (220°C).

Roll Out Pizza Dough:
- Roll out the pizza dough on a floured surface to your desired thickness.

Bake:
- Place the pizza dough on a baking sheet. Bake in the preheated oven until the crust is golden, following the instructions on the pizza dough package.

Spread Avocado Lime Cream:

- Once the pizza crust is baked, spread the avocado lime cream evenly over the crust.

Add Fresh Fruit Toppings:
- Arrange sliced kiwi, strawberries, and bananas over the avocado lime cream.

Optional: Drizzle with Honey:
- Optionally, drizzle a bit of honey over the top for extra sweetness.

Garnish with Mint Leaves:
- Garnish the Avocado Lime Dessert Pizza with fresh mint leaves for a burst of freshness.

Slice and Serve:
- Slice the dessert pizza into portions and serve immediately.

Enjoy the creamy and zesty goodness of Avocado Lime Dessert Pizza! This refreshing dessert is perfect for those who appreciate the unique combination of creamy avocado and citrusy lime. Customize with your favorite fruits and savor this delightful treat.

Cajeta Apple Dessert Pizza

Ingredients:

For the Pizza Dough:

- 1 pizza dough (store-bought or homemade)

For the Cajeta Sauce:

- 1 cup cajeta (Mexican caramel sauce)

For the Apple Topping:

- 2-3 apples, peeled, cored, and thinly sliced
- 2 tablespoons unsalted butter
- 2 tablespoons brown sugar
- 1/2 teaspoon ground cinnamon
- Pinch of salt

For the Cream Cheese Drizzle:

- 4 oz cream cheese, softened
- 1/4 cup powdered sugar
- 1 teaspoon vanilla extract
- 2-3 tablespoons milk

For Garnish:

- Chopped pecans or walnuts
- Dash of ground cinnamon

Instructions:

Preparing the Cajeta Apple Dessert Pizza:

Preheat Oven:
- Preheat your oven according to the pizza dough package instructions or to 425°F (220°C).

Roll Out Pizza Dough:
- Roll out the pizza dough on a floured surface to your desired thickness.

Bake:

- Place the pizza dough on a baking sheet. Bake in the preheated oven until the crust is golden, following the instructions on the pizza dough package.

Prepare Cajeta Sauce:
- Warm the cajeta in a saucepan over low heat until it becomes a pourable consistency. Set aside.

Caramelize Apple Slices:
- In a skillet, melt butter over medium heat. Add thinly sliced apples, brown sugar, ground cinnamon, and a pinch of salt. Cook for 5-7 minutes, stirring occasionally, until the apples are softened and caramelized. Remove from heat.

Prepare Cream Cheese Drizzle:
- In a bowl, beat together softened cream cheese, powdered sugar, vanilla extract, and milk until smooth and creamy. Adjust the consistency by adding more milk if needed.

Assemble the Dessert Pizza:
- Spread the warmed cajeta over the baked pizza crust. Arrange the caramelized apple slices on top.

Drizzle with Cream Cheese Sauce:
- Drizzle the cream cheese sauce over the apple slices.

Optional: Garnish with Nuts and Cinnamon:
- Optionally, sprinkle chopped pecans or walnuts over the pizza. Dust with a dash of ground cinnamon for added flavor.

Slice and Serve:
- Slice the Cajeta Apple Dessert Pizza into portions and serve warm.

Enjoy the rich and indulgent flavors of cajeta, caramelized apples, and cream cheese in this delightful dessert pizza! Customize with additional toppings or a scoop of vanilla ice cream for an extra treat.

Mexican Wedding Cookie Pizza

Ingredients:

For the Cookie Crust:

- 1 cup unsalted butter, softened
- 1/2 cup powdered sugar
- 2 cups all-purpose flour
- 1/2 cup ground almonds or pecans
- 1 teaspoon vanilla extract
- Pinch of salt

For the Toppings:

- Powdered sugar for dusting
- Chopped pecans or almonds for garnish
- Cinnamon for sprinkling

Instructions:

Making the Cookie Crust:

Preheat Oven:
- Preheat your oven to 350°F (180°C).

Cream Butter and Sugar:
- In a large mixing bowl, cream together the softened butter and powdered sugar until light and fluffy.

Add Flour and Nuts:
- Gradually add the all-purpose flour, ground almonds or pecans, vanilla extract, and a pinch of salt. Mix until the dough comes together.

Form Cookie Crust:
- Press the cookie dough into a round shape on a pizza stone or a baking sheet lined with parchment paper. Create a crust by pressing the edges slightly.

Bake:
- Bake in the preheated oven for 20-25 minutes or until the edges are golden brown.

Cool:
- Allow the cookie crust to cool completely before adding toppings.

Adding Toppings:

Dust with Powdered Sugar:
- Once the cookie crust is cool, dust the surface generously with powdered sugar.

Sprinkle Chopped Nuts:
- Sprinkle chopped pecans or almonds over the powdered sugar for added texture.

Optional: Cinnamon Sprinkle:
- Optionally, sprinkle a bit of ground cinnamon over the top for additional flavor.

Slice and Serve:
- Slice the Mexican Wedding Cookie Pizza into wedges and serve.

This Mexican Wedding Cookie Pizza offers the classic flavors of buttery, nutty wedding cookies in a delightful dessert pizza form. Enjoy the sweet simplicity of this treat, perfect for special occasions or any time you crave a delicious and easy-to-share dessert!

Horchata Dessert Pizza

Ingredients:

For the Pizza Dough:

- 1 pizza dough (store-bought or homemade)

For the Horchata Cream Sauce:

- 1 cup sweetened condensed milk
- 1 cup rice milk (homemade or store-bought)
- 1 teaspoon ground cinnamon
- 1 teaspoon vanilla extract
- Pinch of salt

For the Toppings:

- Sliced bananas
- Chopped almonds or horchata-flavored nuts
- Shredded coconut
- Cinnamon sugar for sprinkling

Instructions:

Making the Horchata Cream Sauce:

Prepare Horchata Cream Sauce:
- In a bowl, whisk together sweetened condensed milk, rice milk, ground cinnamon, vanilla extract, and a pinch of salt until well combined. Set aside.

Assembling the Horchata Dessert Pizza:

Preheat Oven:
- Preheat your oven according to the pizza dough package instructions or to 425°F (220°C).

Roll Out Pizza Dough:
- Roll out the pizza dough on a floured surface to your desired thickness.

Bake:
- Place the pizza dough on a baking sheet. Bake in the preheated oven until the crust is golden, following the instructions on the pizza dough package.

Spread Horchata Cream Sauce:
- Once the pizza crust is baked, spread the horchata cream sauce evenly over the crust.

Add Sliced Bananas and Toppings:
- Arrange sliced bananas over the horchata cream sauce. Sprinkle chopped almonds or horchata-flavored nuts and shredded coconut on top.

Optional: Sprinkle with Cinnamon Sugar:
- Optionally, sprinkle cinnamon sugar over the pizza for an extra touch of sweetness.

Slice and Serve:
- Slice the Horchata Dessert Pizza into portions and serve immediately.

Enjoy the rich and cinnamon-infused flavors of horchata in this unique dessert pizza! The combination of creamy horchata sauce, fresh bananas, and crunchy toppings creates a delicious treat reminiscent of the popular Mexican beverage. Customize with your favorite nuts or additional toppings as desired.

www.ingramcontent.com/pod-product-compliance
Lightning Source LLC
LaVergne TN
LVHW081555060526
838201LV00054B/1900